SEASONS OF SOUL

LEADERSHIP LESSONS RECONNECTING OUR WORK, FAMILIES AND COMMUNITIES

SUSAN MOTKALUK

ISBN: 978-1-959993-54-4

Networlding PUBLISHING

CONTENTS

Each season sets its cadence for your life and your life's work. What cadence will you follow with the re-emergence of each season?
The answer to the question above will help you realize the treasures of your life.
Who do you surround yourself with at work, home, and in your community?

What to do in the Spring, Summer, Fall and Winter. What does your seasonal process look like? What does your intentional seasonal process mean to you and those around you?

When you are on the right path, you are being carried. ~ Susan

ACKNOWLEDGMENTS

This book, *Seasons of Soul,* has been a journey of its own, and like any journey, it was not taken alone. I am indebted to the many individuals who have walked alongside me, offering guidance, support, and inspiration.

- **Robbie and Cash:** Your curiosity and boundless energy have been a constant reminder of the simple joys and profound truths of life. You are my greatest inspirations.
- **Melissa G Wilson, My Publisher:** Thank you for supporting my vision and for giving me the opportunity to share this specialized knowledge with the world so that it may benefit as many people as possible.
- **The University of Waterloo:** For giving me a chance to change my life.
- **Charlie LaLonde:** Your wisdom and guidance have shaped my path in more ways than I can articulate. Thank you for always challenging me to seek a deeper truth.
- **Chuck Homer:** For being a guiding light when I needed it most on my TEC coaching journey.
- **Bruce and Sharon Vandenberg:** For believing in me.
- **Marshall Goldsmith:** For inspiring me, believing in me, and showing me the stakeholder-centered certified way.
- **My Influences:** To all the great writers and

philosophers whose work has touched me and influenced me, both creatively and in life.

- **Mother Nature:** For providing me with the seasonal changes I could always count on, the constant in my life.

"*Seasons of Soul* is a beautifully written reflection on life, leadership, and the rhythm that connects them both. Susan Motkaluk blends the wisdom of nature with the lessons of resilience, guiding readers to find balance, meaning, and renewal in every stage of their personal and professional lives. With grace and grounded insight, she reminds us that growth isn't a race—it's a cycle. This book is a compass for anyone seeking to live and lead with purpose, clarity, and heart."

Dr. Marshall Goldsmith is the *Thinkers50* #1 Executive Coach and New York Times bestselling author of *The Earned Life*, *Triggers*, and *What Got You Here Won't Get You There*.

INTRODUCTION

Every season allows you to find a tempo—a rhythm for living and working, just like Earth's tilted axis allows for the natural rhythm of life on our planet. That oscillation provides a solid axis for our own lives. Why? The Earth's spin axis is tilted, causing different parts of the planet to receive more direct sunlight at other times of the year as it orbits the Sun. The remarkable nature of seasonal change allows us to adapt to the many new options each season provides.

After more than 200 seasonal changes, their power offers us continual shifts and, if chosen, improvements in not only our personal lives but also our family lives, business lives, and spiritual lives. Seasons provide us with truly soulful interludes of change and growth. This is why I have divided this book into seasons.

By offering you a quarterly framework that follows the circular, self-renewing rhythm of nature, I will show you how the many lessons I have created over the years can offer you a rare opportunity: the chance to live your life *with* and *in touch* with nature itself. Don't worry. I'll show you how to do this. It will make for a beautiful new lifestyle. How do I know? I'm happy to share my experience with you.

I grew up in the smallest mountain town in Canada. There, I learned from the land and the seasons, along with the wisdom of my family and the meager lifestyle that challenged me to reach for more, first for myself and later for my two amazing sons.

If you think about it, our lives have a profound discrepancy. We are born. Then, we enter this race to improve constantly until we die. Yet every day we are presented with examples of a different way of living within a seasonal context. For example, trees grow leaves and then shed them, only to bloom again. Just as we do, animals and plants also follow a continuous cycle, a cycle we continually strive to emulate and adapt to our linear thinking.

Let me show you how to align with the natural cycle of life instead—how to learn from the millennia of wisdom around us.

Life teaches us many lessons. While not all lessons are pleasant, they are often essential for understanding the bigger picture and helping you move forward through challenging times. We learn our lessons through personal experiences—mistakes, failures, obstacles, and painful confrontations — that enable us to acquire knowledge that would be difficult to attain otherwise. Many of these lessons are worth revisiting or remembering forever.

During my childhood, I grew up primarily barefoot and poor. This created powerful, life-altering experiences that set the stage for me to become the strong, resilient person I am today. As a result of those formative years, I can now share many experiences, lessons learned, and insights with you to help you reach for more than you ever thought possible and achieve far more than you think you can.

I am grateful that I learned these lessons early in life. My greatest hope is that you, too, will gain from my experiences.

You, too, will learn to lean in and out from the sun, finding your unique rhythm in this dance of life.

This book blends natural laws with solid leadership lessons to build robust community, family, and workplace connections. If COVID-19 taught us anything, it is that we should not forsake our personal lives and lean too heavily on our business lives, becoming unbalanced.

I like to think of the special wisdom some of us learn and even master along our life journey. These I refer to as "ornaments." They weave like gossamer threads into the rich tapestry of one's life, and they're essential to living and creating a community of support and a life well-lived, both at work and at home.

If you think about it, there's a discrepancy in our lives—

A Childhood Devoid of Rhythm

Let me go back even further so you can better understand where I came from and the path I took to get to where I am today. It all began back in rural Canada.

I was born in St. Rose Du Lac, and I have no idea why. We didn't even live there. As with most of my childhood, it occurred with no rhyme or reason. This randomness of events brings with it a fractured understanding of my past. It is why I felt lost and confused for most of my early years.

My parents each left their respective farms in the Rural Municipality of Mountain for a better life. There are fewer than 1500 people in the RM of Mountain, 1500 sq km. The community was paramount in that place. It was you and the neighbors. You do one un-neighborly thing, and it can entrench your family into generations of unnecessary difficulty. You can imagine the pressure of being a good, wholesome part of the community and what that kind of pressure means for the children. The Motkaluk family, my family, had a good name in Manitoba, and that mattered.

My dad's family farms are incredibly beautiful and rough at the same time. My mom's family farm home was a beautiful, tidy wooden house, painted white, with a white picket fence and a majestic, sturdy barn that my grandfather built. The yard was neat, and the fields were beautiful beyond anything you could imagine.

Behind the house ran a frigid, murky creek. There was even a genuine hand pump for pumping water and an icebox with a block of ice. Amazingly, those farms are still in the family.

For me, growing up here meant wild horses and oil lamps. It also meant fantastic work and many amazing natural lessons to be learned: tall grasses and majestic trees, berries, and mushrooms. I remember going mushroom picking and getting lost, picking wild berries, and eating them faster than I chose them.

Memories of getting lost in the tall grass, building forts in it, and later learning how terrible it was to do so were also part of my childhood. Smells play a significant role in our lives; for me, the smell of freshly cut hay is the anchor to where I came from.

I have fragments of memories from that time. There was Mrs. Wishard. She made dolls, and they were beautiful. And Mr. McEwen had decorations for every holiday. No matter how much or how little anyone had, the community was close. Everyone knew everyone and everything—a blessing and a curse.

I still remember the light green wooden house where we lived in Dauphin. It was always filled with the clamor of shouting matches, of friends and neighbors constantly stopping by. To me, it was never a home. It was more like a way station, a very *temporary* place, so temporary that I lived daily waiting for another upheaval. Amidst all the drama, I never felt safe. Instead, I focused on identifying a future role in which I could create and control a better environment—a safer one.

Sometimes, I thought those green, wooden walls protected me. Most of the time, though, I was scared and lonely.

In those wild childhood years, I reminded myself of a rabbit, always on the lookout, ready to jump away from danger.

My memory could be better, though. I guess it's a consequence of shutting things out to survive and keep moving forward. But there are memories I cherish from that time, as they give me a better sense of myself:

A word on structure

Let's talk a bit about what you can expect from this book.

We start our journey through the seasons of the soul with spring. It's the season of rejuvenation, of springing forward, of finding our new selves–I thought it only appropriate to begin where Mother Nature herself seems to be beginning.

Although we may think we have moved away from nature, our lives are still governed by natural laws — the laws of survival, rhythm, and energy. I kick-start every season by reminding myself of those laws. They are essential in understanding what each part of the year can teach us.

There are three parts to each season. The same parts of our lives are made up of family, work, and community. Through a cornucopia of memories, lessons, distilled experiences, and fun stories, I guide us from the house's enclosure to the broader horizons of work and into our final destination, the community of human beings who surround and define us.

Each season concludes with a leadership lesson and a brief takeaway note. Leadership is present in all seasons of business life. Journey through each season of the year and build on your traditions, habits, and rituals. Find your cadence, work hard, play hard, and dig deep. Then celebrate, pause, and reflect. Rinse and repeat; consistency matters. *Stick and stay and make it pay.*

Transcendence

> You must take personal responsibility. You cannot change the circumstances, the seasons, or the wind, but you can change yourself. That is something you have charge of.
>
> —JIM ROHN

There are moments when a seismic disruption occurs that, on the outside, looks like a total failure, but that eventually provides the clarity that aligns you with your optimal destiny.

PRELUDE: CIRCLES

> "It's the circle of life, and it moves us all through despair and hope, through faith and love, 'til we find our place on the path unwinding."
>
> — ELTON JOHN (*THE CIRCLE OF LIFE* FROM *THE LION KING*, 1994)

> "Life is a circle. The end of one journey is the beginning of the next."
>
> — JOSEPH M. MARSHALL III

Through my life experiences, I have learned several ways to counter this growing epidemic inherent in natural laws: the rhythm of the four seasons, the time-tested methods of Canada's Indigenous peoples, and the traditions of many other cultures that have left an imprint on me.

In today's fast-paced society, how do you reconnect? How do we combat loneliness?

One method is to apply the concept of circles.

The power of circles rests in their very nature. Everything is cyclical: the four seasons, the rotation of the Earth and the Moon, the rise and fall of the tides, and a person's life from birth to death. Not only are circles inherently balanced and equal, but we are all equal within a circle.

Therefore, many restorative and therapy groups and practices, from Indigenous Healing Circles to Alcoholics Anonymous, meet in a circle. The circle's equality comes from the fact that no one is in front of you, no one is behind you, no one is above or below you. They implicitly assign value to every member of the circle.

By aligning our lives with the natural world's cycles, we can gain powerful lessons.

In my opinion and experience, I love the whole idea of circles. If a circle is closed, it keeps everything connected. It's a closed loop. When it's circular, everything is working. It ebbs, it flows, it moves, it's supported, and it's vital. The idea of the circle of life reminds us that our lives continually renew, revitalize, and that the seasons always run their course. The sun will always rise and set.[1]

If the circle opens up and brings in, let's say, a new person, family, or a piece of the puzzle, it's acceptable. That circle absorbs it, incorporates it, and it becomes part of the circle. That's a natural way that a circle can open and embrace. Now it's a slightly bigger circle, but it's still one intact circle.

When the circle is broken - like an epidemic out there - there's just no strength. There's no support, no ebb, no flow. There's just

---

1. Covalent Logic Website. "The Circle of Life: A Roundup of Interpretations." covalentlogic.com. April 23, 2019. https://www.covalentlogic.com/news/529

no rhythm that works because it's like a bridge to nowhere. It goes nowhere. The energy just stops. It's open, and then it just falls off the cliff.

> "Will the circle be unbroken
>
> By and by, Lord, by and by."
>
> — ADA R. HABERSHON AND CHARLES H. GABRIEL

When you think about a car tire, if the wheel is broken, it won't roll. You can't roll down the highway. In Manitoba, people stop to help out a driver stuck on the side of the road. In Toronto, nobody stops. They can't. You'd be killed. They're entirely immobilized because they have a flat tire. It could be the smallest thing. It could just be a nail in the tire, and it stops you completely. When someone or something breaks the circle, nothing works.

That's a higher concept. When you're looking to reconnect with work, family, or community, it is about creating a cohesive circle that can feed off one another, thrive, and support one another. There's energy and strength with the circle. Loneliness is an epidemic. You feel lonely at work, you feel lonely at home, you feel lonely when you're out.

My mom lived in a small village with fewer than fifty permanent residents. Yet whenever I went there, I felt surrounded by people, and I was never lonely. If I walked down the street, people would talk to me and ask how I was doing.

When I first moved to Toronto, I called my mom and said, "I've never been so lonely in all my life, in a sea of millions of people. Nobody talked to me today." I kept track of it in a diary, and the longest I went without anybody acknowledging me or saying hi was two weeks. I would say hello to them, but in Toronto, for me, that was considered really unusual. If you say hello to someone, they very often will not say hello back.

Coming from friendly Manitoba, we acknowledged everybody. I found this really interesting, having never experienced this before. You could go the whole day without an invitation or even a "How are you?" It was the loneliest I have ever felt.

Cultural norms, traditions, and community have sustained circles. I had no sense of community. I had no strong circles.

Reconnecting families, communities, and work will rely on the notion of a circle, forming strong circles, and acknowledging them. When you look at the seasons, if you really think about it, they're circles. The rotation of the Earth. Why are the seasons changing? The way the sun tilts back and forth. It's all circular.

We once lived in a society that placed immense priority on family and community. But over time, we have become more self-centered. When we are more focused on work and ourselves, we feel alone despite being surrounded by many people.

Even in a densely populated city, we can feel utterly alone. We go unseen. People no longer know their neighbours. People are less likely to stop and help someone they pass by.

We must work hard to create our own circles. Find a circle, and contribute to it. Be proactive. Join a group of people with shared values and shared interests. Work towards a common goal. Any goal, large or small. Joining a community garden to help feed the less fortunate, or even something as trivial as doll collecting or knitting. Find your circle. This will give you a sense of belonging and remind you that you are not alone. Leadership circles and peer groups are extremely powerful.

There's a natural rhythm in the seasons, and it is a circular rhythm. It's the idea that spring will return. Spring will come back because it's in the circle. You'll see spring again. It will be slightly different, but it will come again. Fall will come again.

The notion of the seasons and recognizing that there's a natural cadence in your life, one that you should respect and acknowledge. Furthermore, the best way to connect those circles is through habits, traditions, beliefs, and cultural practices. These factors are all very important for forming a circle. People will gather. Ideally, people will gather repeatedly. Every time will be slightly different, and we will have marginally deeper connections.

Let's take a look at your work meetings. Businesses that operate effectively have regular touchpoints. For example, we meet every Tuesday and Thursday for 15 minutes every morning. We hold weekly and quarterly meetings and, in addition, form habits of acknowledging one another, sharing meals, or celebrating successes.

Meet. Meet again. Share. Share again. Next thing you know, you are together, seated, and easily propelled forward.

Again, all of that ties back into this circle-forming process. You build on that. You say, "This is what we always do. These are the expectations. This is how this company has formed and functions." Typically, people know what to expect and feel comfortable, strong, and not alone. The same thing happens in families and communities.

The idea of connectedness is really what makes you strong. Suppose you go back to nature, which is again back to the seasons. If you were standing in the forest all by yourself 1,000 years ago, it was not a safe thing to do. These communities and these families were strongest when they were together. That just ties into the circle. The cadence of the seasons and being cognizant of these natural laws, bring those circles back into focus. Have intent.

A few words on natural law. Numerous definitions exist on the topic. In philosophy, it is considered a "...system of right or justice held to be common to all humans and derived from nature rather than from the rules of society, or positive law."[2] Another aspect is natural law moral theory, which states that the moral standards that govern human behavior are objectively derived from the nature of human beings and the nature of the world.[3]

St. Thomas Aquinas wrote prolifically on the subject, stating, "The light of reason is placed by nature [and thus by God] in every man to guide him in his acts."[4] His conclusion was that of all God's creatures, solely human beings employ reason to lead their lives, and that was Aquinas's definition of natural law. He believed that we are naturally rational beings; therefore, it is morally appropriate for humans to act in ways that conform to their rational nature.

This epidemic of loneliness, the unnecessary hardships people face at work, the strained family dynamics, and the declining communities simply bring back the circle. Just acknowledge it. Do it with intent. Do it as a practice. Just give it a try and see what happens.

My children are very aware of "This is what we always do."

---

2. Britannica Website. "Natural Law: Definition." Britannica.com. Accessed June 4, 2022. https://www.britannica.com/topic/natural-law
3. Internet Encyclopedia of Philosophy. "Natural Law." IEP. Accessed June 4, 2022. https://iep.utm.edu/natlaw/#:~:text=According%20to%20natural%20law%20moral,the%20nature%20of%20the%20world.
4. Constitutional Rights Foundation Website. "St. Thomas Aquinas, Natural Law, and the Common Good." CRF-USA.org. Accessed June 4, 2022.https://www.crf-usa.org/bill-of-rights-in-action/bria-22-4-c-st-thomas-aquinas-natural-law-and-the-common-good

They have come to rely on it and derive considerable comfort from it. We still do exciting and new things, but we always go to the same place at the same time and see the same people. It gives them a sense of belonging and strength, and they don't feel alone.

They walk around with confidence. I know their peers look at them and think, "How are you so confident? Why are you so at ease?" Because they know that they are a part of something bigger than they are. They're part of a bigger circle. In fact, they are part of a seasonal circle.

We have a big family. I always make a point of gathering with them. Even if we fight, we meet anyway. Even if we're strained, we still get together. And if things are difficult, the credo is, "Well, we have to meet because it's Christmas. We always meet at Christmas." Or, "We have to meet because we always meet for the boys' birthdays." That's the point. We come together regardless, because of the tradition, habit, or the cultural norm, or whatever you want to call it. That's what constantly brings you together.

Why do people like to gather? If I invite people to my parties, why do they all come? Because they know what to expect. We always have fun. I like to include an eclectic mix of newcomers to broaden the circle. We do have some base traditions, but we always make room for new people. We set a place for a stranger.

Coming back full circle

Remember when I told you I was born in a random town—another example of how my childhood was devoid of rhythm? Even a broken clock, though, is right twice a day.

As it turned out, I was born in a blessed town. It features a grotto that is an authentic replica of the Notre-Dame of Lourdes. The cave was built as a religious shrine, and I am certain it was consecrated, which means a whole lot more than I even know. Luckily, this blessing rubbed off on me.

I have had considerable good fortune and have overcome many odds. My lot in life was predetermined. If I had tried, worked hard, and been lucky, I could have been a waitress and owned a dilapidated house in rural Manitoba. Neglect and poverty do shape a person in a good way and in a bad way. The way I saw it, being the only sibling born in this grotto town gave me a superb chance of beating some odds—or so I believed.

I visited the grotto before I entered engineering school, and it was there that I told myself to go and never look back. I visited it several times after university and again with my young children. I sat and prayed while the boys ran all around. As I sat there, I said to myself that my boys would never understand my lot in life and how I broke the generational chains so they could be ignorant of how impossible my life once was.

In the end, though, anything could have been my grotto—I could have even built one myself. And I would love to help you make your own—for your business, for your life, for your people.

SPRING

Spring

Sound the flute!
Now it's mute!
Bird's delight,
Day and night,
Nightingale,
In the dale,
Lark in the Sky—
Merrily,
Merrily, merrily, to welcome in the year.

Little boy,
Full of joy;
Little girl,
Sweet and small;
Cock does crow,
So do you;.Merry voice,
Infant noise;
Merrily, merrily, to welcome in the year.

Little lamb,
Here I am;
Come and lick
My white neck;
Let me pull
Your soft wool;
Let me kiss
Your soft face;
Merrily, merrily, we welcome in the year.

~ William Blake,[1]
from his book *Songs of Innocence*, published in 1789

I share this sweet old poem to illustrate that spring is a time of renewal and to remind you that even in business, the seasons of growth ebb and flow. There are fluctuations in the business cycle. For example, during spring, we create business plans and roll out new products and services, and the marketing department comes up with new designs.[2]

In her blog post for "We Are Wildness", Shelley O'Connell shares how Native Americans know each season has unique attributes and lessons to nourish you and your life. Here is an excerpt from that post:

"Let's start with the East. This is the Spring. It is the place of new beginnings, the dawn of a new day, and birth. This season is represented by the color yellow, like the sunrise."

She goes on to compare babies' qualities, such as trust, wonder,

---

1. Blake, William. "Spring." Poetry Lovers Page. Accessed June 9, 2022. https://www.poetryloverspage.com/poets/blake/spring.html
2. Brodie, Peter. "The Four Seasons of Business: Why Spring is Around the Corner." Forbes. June 18, 2020. https://www.forbes.com/sites/forbescoachescouncil/2020/06/18/the-four-seasons-of-business-why-spring-is-around-the-corner/?sh=7250a4106787

vulnerability, and more, which can be either discovered or reclaimed during spring. She further argues that, for babies, flora, and fauna to flourish, they require care and nurturance. Shelley encourages you to do the same for yourself, as well as for your ideas, hopes, and dreams that you hope to create and grow in spring.

Introduction to Spring

Spring has a way of making our hearts sing after the long, dark winter months. There is such delight in spotting the first crocus, a telltale sign that the earth is awakening from its slumber. Life starts to vibrate and pulsate with excitement. The quiet that characterized winter is broken by returning birds, the scuttling of animals, and the sounds of people enjoying the outdoors as they emerge from hibernation.

The quality of enthusiasm facilitates engaging with and enjoying the movement of our bodies. It is wonderful to enjoy the outdoors with our families as we look forward to the rest of the year. Although spring has a light-hearted quality, it is also when seeds are sown for future harvests.

Gardens do not magically provide us with bounty. They require planning and work, much of which occurs in the spring. Nature's freshness can also inspire our business activities if we learn to listen to its cues.

Spring is about rebirth... rebirth in the trees as they bud forth another new year of life. It is about the sun, which offers deep warmth to the bright, rich, and blossoming flowers, sparkling with the colors orange, yellow, purple, and blue, popping up and dazzling us with their beauty.

. . .

The arrival of spring brings more daylight, and the increased light increases serotonin levels, which makes us feel happier. It's a new beginning of a whole new cycle, breathing new life into old projects, broken initiatives, and stalled efforts. Spring brings an opportunity to develop new energy and focus with new tactics that will result in a rebirth of you, your organization, your family, and your community.

Here are a few more thoughts on Spring

Michael Tompkins, a San Francisco-based psychologist and author, notes that "We live in an acquiring culture, and perhaps there are some of us, myself included, that long for the serenity that can come with less stuff." He has written books on hoarding, and his view that doing some spring cleaning and purging emphasizes the credo "Less is more" is excellent.

Regina Leeds,[3] a professional organizer and NY Times best-seller, adds, "We can calm the inside by bringing order to the outer." Spring cleaning creates an authentic "fresh start" effect, similar to the feeling we get from setting New Year's resolutions (and then *acting* upon them).

Therefore, Spring itself embodies an incredibly dynamic fresh start potential. In fact, clutter can be a major contributor to stress. Research studies have shown that clutter and procrastination negatively affect well-being, particularly among women. These can actually induce a physiological response—including higher levels of cortisol, our primary stress hormone.[4]

As we delve further into this lovely season, we'll explore other

---

3. Ibid.
4. Lucchesi, Emilie le Beau. "The Unbearable Heaviness of Clutter." New York Times. January 3, 2019. https://www.nytimes.com/2019/01/03/well/mind/clutter-stress-procrastination-psychology.html

activities that spring lends its amazing energy to. As I've been writing this, some of my early childhood memories have come rushing back, just like the freshness of Spring.

My Memories of Spring

Mrs Wishard

One of my earliest childhood memories was walking down a dirt path to Mrs. Wishard's back steps in Ochre River, climbing those steps, and stepping into her house. I remember exploring her home, a tidy, wooden-framed house, and in every room I entered, there were dolls. Mrs. Wishard made these dolls by hand. I could not believe it.

To my surprise, she even had a doll in her bathroom, a pretty face with dark brown hair and a red-and-white crocheted dress. The dress had a full, puffy skirt, and the doll stood neatly on the back of the toilet shelf. Under the beautiful skirt of the doll's dress, a roll of toilet paper. I was totally awestruck. How on earth did she think to make that doll? And to think, even her toilet paper was prettied up. As I left Mrs. Wishard's house, I remember licking my finger and dipping it into the fancy sugar bowl she had out on the table, and the sugar stuck to the tip of my finger, and as I ran out the back door, I sucked that sugar right off my finger: a wonderful experience and a wonderful memory.

Parades

If there was anything that symbolized the coming together of our community, it was the Ukrainian Festival Parade. Everyone lined the streets, and I mean everyone, from the oldest to the youngest. We sat on the curb and waited for the parade to come our way. I could not believe the thundering music of the marching bands and the roar of the sirens. And of course, the horses.

One of my favorite aspects of this parade was the clowns and floats that would throw candy to the observers. I got to grab as much as I could. It was amazing... getting totally lost in the wonderment of the moment, letting go of anything sad or difficult. My cheeks would hurt from smiling and laughing. With the sensory overload of the colorful clothing and the sounds of the marching band, somehow I magically ceased being a lonely little girl. That aspect of me dissolved. I became one of the many, and that collective experience was profound.

My dad built us a playhouse in 1971 in Ochre River. It was a simple wooden house, with boards 4 feet wide and 88 feet long, which avoided excessive wood cutting. It resembled a gingerbread house, complete with a large pink heart at the peak of the roof. At that time, my dad was a teacher, and he had the kids from his class come and paint murals inside the playhouse.

I remember one wall depicting The Three Little Pigs, and on the ceiling, the cow jumping over the moon. Even the Big Bad Wolf was painted on one wall, and it was excellent. My dad brought the playhouse with us from Ochre River to Dauphin, and later on to Selkirk, and then to Matheson.

That playhouse won first prize in the Dauphin Santa Claus parade. It is a fond memory. When we lost the Matheson house along with the playhouse, the economy was reeling out of control, as was our family. Some families could weather these difficult economic times, but without a strong team, we didn't stand a chance. We were constantly broke.

But the parades were reliable. They were larger than life and conveyed a sense of community and coming together that was much broader than my own life at home.

Our Green Wooden House

In Dauphin, Manitoba, everyone knew everyone. Our wooden house was light green and had both a front and a backyard. Smoke filled the air, and the loud noises and the high energy of family, friends, and neighbors stopping by the house filled the rooms, so I wouldn't call it home. Sometimes, I did think we were cool. But most of the time, I was scared and lonely.

Although we lived on Main Street, we also had a backyard and a front yard. I had the most amazing doll named Mrs. Beasley. She was a character doll based on the housekeeper from the sitcom *Family Affair*. She had glasses, and when you pulled her string, she talked, of course, saying the same phrases over and over. I loved her. I took her everywhere—to the shop-easy and the book nook.

I vividly remember going places by myself back then, which is unusual given that I was probably less than 5 years old, likely as young as 2 or 3. Neglect does funny things to your brain and your heart. I usually wore pigtails or a ponytail. I always tried to present myself well, as being looked down on by others always made me uncomfortable.

My mom was already exhibiting signs of profound depression. I would often say, "She just doesn't care like the other moms do." There were no discernible signs of maternal instincts. She was sometimes kind to babies, although it was clear that she did not like older kids.

I was outside one night, sleeping on my tricycle with a pillow on the handlebars. Of course, I had done this many times and mastered it. Suddenly, I realized I could not find Mrs. Beasley. There was no snow on the ground, and it was warm enough without a jacket. I had no shoes on. I remember looking frantically, crying, and screaming for my doll. For sure, it was well past 10 p.m. What the hell was I doing outside?

Well, I alarmed the neighborhood. Everyone came running, and, typical of our community, they all helped me find my doll. My mom and dad had excellent explanations for why I was such an unreasonable, typical small child.

This moment was one of the rare times in my life when I saw people genuinely care. Everyone looked for the doll as though I mattered. They found her, and all was good in my world once again. I remember thinking, "Why is everyone doing this for me?" The kindness of the neighborhood shone through, making me really notice how important a community can be. It helps you feel like you're truly a part of something special. This experience showed me what it meant to rely on others, something that my family had failed to teach me.

Back inside the house on Main Street, you can imagine what I faced after bringing that much attention to my fragile family. They quickly reminded me to shut the hell up.

Trains and Bullies

When I was a child, I was bullied frequently. I looked disheveled daily. I had no one at home to help me be presentable. So I just went to school in dirty clothes, messy hair, and no coat or good shoes. I also often didn't have food or school supplies. There was no question. I was an easy target.

Sometimes teachers would help, such as by brushing my hair, but mostly I felt judged and afraid. I couldn't stand up for myself for a long time.

My sister and I had to walk to school daily on train tracks. We often heard stories of kids getting hurt or killed by a train.

Danger was constant, so much so that the memories of those days still haunt me.

The bullies would also often chase my sister and me on the railroad tracks, throwing rocks. Once, a rock hit me in the ear. I started thinking of ways to outsmart them to survive.

Once, a teacher reported the bullying to the principal. I had to report what was happening, and the main bully was disciplined. But then he beat me up worse, so I never told again.

I decided I had to figure out how to deal with bullies on my own, without asking for help. I'm still like that today.

Conclusions:

1. Bullies pick on kids who look neglected or different.
2. Being poor and neglected made school life really hard.
3. I faced danger every day just getting to school.
4. Telling adults about bullying doesn't always help and can make things worse.
5. I learned to rely on myself to solve problems by building a strong friend group.
6. Childhood experiences can affect you for a long time.

Lesson Learned

I was determined to outrun, outsmart, and outmaneuver these bullies. I also found out that if I surround myself with strong friends, life was easier, more fun, and more interesting.

Family

At last! Spring is here. There is even a spring in your step and a glint in your eye. You can see the dirt differently. You start to notice things that don't look right, the ones that don't fit in. Time to sweep out the cobwebs. Get to work on everything. Nature is awakening. This is a time for you to reset, rebirth, and rejoice; your family life will also have a certain exciting dynamic.

Family Activities to Share, even if You're on a Shoestring Budget

Not everything worthwhile costs much money. The best things in life are free, right? Regardless of your family's budget, here are a few suggestions that you can enjoy together to celebrate Spring!

During one of those legendary April showers that bring May flowers, go outside and play in the rain! Jump in puddles, catch raindrops on your tongues, and encourage one another to describe what the falling rain sounds, feels, looks, and smells like

Plant a vegetable and/or flower garden. What better way to allow Mother Nature to do her thing and share her bounty with your family?

Take a nature walk or go on a family bike ride.

Become a "twitcher." This is what the British call birdwatchers. Encourage your family members to learn to identify different birds by their appearance as well as their unique songs. Research what types of materials local birds use for building their nests, and leave some of these items outside to help them create their Spring homes.

I did a bird study in University and sat in the same spot, at the same time every day. I counted the birds I saw and identified the species. I loved it. The activity was freeing and fun.

Participate in as many free outdoor concerts and community events as possible.

These are simply a few ideas. Create as many as possible for your family.

The Three Blooms: A Garden-Based Plan for Lasting Change

> We might think we are nurturing our garden, but of course, it's our garden that is really nurturing us.
>
> —JENNY UGLOW

My favorite thing to do is to sit in my old Victorian garden, listening to Nina Simone's *Feeling Good.* I didn't plant the garden. Someone else did, 100 years ago. I just get to enjoy it. It blooms every spring in a dance of colors, and by Mother's Day, my garden has come back to life. It never fails me.

It screams at me, "JOY!" No matter what, "JOY". It will return next year. This has been such an important lesson in my life, that permanence, that hope. It is what has enabled me to tap into my own joy, share it, and help change people's lives.

The way it works is this: We use the garden as a measuring stick, a measure of time.

It will take you three garden blooms to change your life if you start now.

Here is my suggestion: Sit in the garden (or anywhere else that is filled with wonder and beauty for you) and declare what you want. Imagine outcomes and success. You develop a loose plan and then work on it throughout the year. Then, come back to the garden in the following spring and report back: What has changed, what has happened, what worked well, and what didn't? Rinse and repeat—consistency and perseverance matter.

Stick and stay and make it pay. Never give up. Three garden blooms later, you will have moved mountains. Rise and do it all over again.

Tips for Spring Rejuvenation

Spring clean. Purge, sort, tidy, repair, repaint, and refresh at the workplace and home. Your space should be refreshing.

Look for signs of spring. Go on a nature walk with your kids and family. Bring your work team outside; do a fun spring project, collect leaves and pieces of nature like buds or foliage, make a spring bouquet, and bring it into the office or home. Take photographs and videos that exhibit the signs of spring, and create a narrative of what you see, touch, feel, and hear. Be inspired.

Take your family somewhere cool. These could be short day trips, staycations, or spring break trips somewhere exotic. Just make sure you take a break. Make sure to look for signs of spring and note them.

Celebrate. Create a special themed celebration for Spring. Celebrations build connections, which help create trust, which helps build confidence, and confident employees create confident customers.

Bring your family together at least once to mark the moment and take notice that spring is in the air.

Work:

"With your personal life feeling refreshed, Spring's energy is perfectly suited to a crucial task in your professional life: Building and energizing your team."

Build your team. Spring is about refocusing and resetting. This is a good time for talent disruption, resetting and rebuilding. Build the right team now.

Revise old projects and initiatives, assign a new team to them, and start again.

Visit, tour, and share a meal.

Inspire and motivate: coach, mentor, support, and encourage new ideas

Conduct a two-day off-site workshop.

Do an environmental scan of all projects underway since the winter. Dump and clean up anything that is not working. Amend budgets and scopes, and reset and refocus the team.

Celebrate! Create a special themed celebration for Spring. Celebrations build connections, connections foster trust, and trust builds confidence; confident employees create confident customers.

Find the new rhythm of Spring.

Go outside and put your bare feet in the grass. Feel the dew on your toes. Connect again, and live life with a spring rhythm. Listen to the 'Spring' movement from Vivaldi's Four Seasons. Be aware that spring is literally in the air. Spend as many days as possible outside. Doing so will reintegrate you back into nature.

It will also help you to re-inspire yourself to grow new seeds of possibility. It will set up a cadence of confidence. Watch the sunlight shift. Look every day for more signs of Spring. Deep clean your home, car, office, and everything. Challenge and involve your family members and your colleagues at work to share what they saw, smelled, heard, or touched today. Embrace every element of Spring, those signs of rebirth that joyfully whisper, "Awaken, awaken!"

Spring is a time of action. Put that action to work, and come summer and fall, you will reap the benefits. But which way should you move? Act, yes, but how?

Apply spring's laws and rhythms to your work, even if you're only just starting or have an empire to run.

The following are practical tools and ideas for applying the wisdom of the youngest season in your workplace.

It's the season to touch, smell, look, and feel—Get out there.

Yes, get out there and "Make Things Happen." It's here that I lead my team on a two- or three-day off-site workshop. Why? Thus, they too can let everything go, focus on the present moment, and tap into spring's excitement.

Innovation, manifestation, and globalization are key concepts I cover at these workshops. Why? Because ideas matter. Some of the best ideas come in the spring because of the energy shift, though you have to slow down long enough to notice. As I say, you need to slow down long enough for life to catch up with you in the winter and the spring. You need to lean in and make things happen.

Embrace spring and apply its lessons at work: Send employees outside with their phones as a small-team project. The team must walk together: one person takes the photos, and the other narrates. Another person selects the background music and edits. The task: showcase signs of spring and connect them to an area where the company can perform better or differently, or identify a dormant project and propose a new approach, including actions to reinvigorate it.

They have 30 minutes to walk and explore, followed by 30 minutes to make final edits. Bring them back into the workshop and ask them to show their videos to everyone. We have better creative energy together. We need to harness it and create a new way of looking at things. Sunshine, foliage, fresh air and water help.

Gather images and videos and combine them. Tell a story of new energy, rebirth, joy, and love. Much is happening outside in the spring, yet we're all too often choosing to remain indoors, failing to observe and engage with it. These things are happening, anyway. Why not harness that energy and put it to good use? Even though things seem to be standing still, they are not. For instance, butterflies, birds, and other organisms are migrating to new climates and habitats. Why not follow their example?

Give your business a fresh start, and people will notice

Imagine what Spring smells, looks, feels, and sounds like. Go outside, connect with Mother Nature the way you did as a child, and live life with a spring rhythm. For instance, look for clouds that resemble pictures of animals or other images. With this renewed energy, you'll light up your team and your company. Your customers will notice something different is underway, and new things are happening.

The effort you make to breathe new life into old things makes people take notice. They'll say and think, "Hey! What is happening with this business? Something new is obviously coming. Everything old is new again, but with a twist. New and fresh. And I like it!"

A Season to Breathe Life into Old Things

Move old projects forward: When spring is in the air, I challenge my teams to wrap their arms around stagnant projects and initiatives that are stuck and breathe new life into them. This heavy lifting will bear fruit. I am gently and sometimes fiercely firing up the energy.

Get out of the office: Have a team BBQ. Go where the people are. Go on a ride-along. Tour. Explore. Tour your jurisdiction. Get out of your office. See your employees, customers, family, and community. Just listen, look, touch, feel, and sprinkle seeds of inspiration and bread-crumb ideas, ask and listen.

Walk around with a coffee cup and observe (you'll read more about the Coffee Cup game later in the Summer section). By being casual yet present, you can learn a lot. Be motivational, inspiring, and above everything, get out of the way, let things happen as they should, and they will.

Inspire: Make sure you feed and water all projects, initiatives, and teams so they can prosper and grow. Your job is to inspire, mentor, coach, feed, and water. Do not starve your team. What can you do better or differently? Convey a clear vision. Be inspiring. Set the course. Assemble the team. Get the resources in place, and get the hell out of the way! Gently guide when necessary.

And don't forget: trust the process.

Spring cleaning is not just for the house. Now is a good time to let go of those who are not stepping up to meet the requirements of their workloads.

It is also a time to hire new personnel. Change is good.

Plant new ideas and nurture them to reap the rewards that unfold.

Some days are diamonds and some days are dust. It is okay. Clean the cobwebs out of the tall corners of your office and your mind. This will make anything that doesn't work stand out. You will want to address it as soon as possible.

Clean out the dust and let the diamonds around you sparkle even more.

Here are some ways I've discovered to help your "diamond" qualities shine brightly:

Stick and stay and make it pay.

Check yourself before you wreck yourself.

Take a bath. Start fresh. Focus on the future.

Don't suck the wind out of anyone's sails.

Lift that wet blanket off, and let your light shine brightly.

They've got a hole in their bucket. No matter how much you give, it all drains out the bottom. You gotta fix the hole first before you can make a difference.

Don't be a bucket dipper.

Guess what happens when you kick a bag of shit? You get shit on your foot.

Don't spread seeds of negativity; they will come back to you.

See the invisible, do the impossible.

Remember you have friends: integrity, perseverance, and consistency. They will all serve you well.

Spring is the best time to make a career move.

If you're thinking about applying for a new job, there's no time like the present. According to *Career Sidekick*, the spring months are some of the best times to make a career move. This is because employers are eager to lock in new hires before Memorial Day. After Memorial Day, summer vacations often make it difficult to efficiently move through the hiring process.

If you're looking for a new job, Liz Wessel, the 26-year-old co-founder and CEO of WayUp, has three tips for you.

1. Don't pigeonhole yourself

"Be open to different types of opportunities," says Wessel. She believes too many recent grads overlook their perfect role by limiting themselves to a specific job title or particular industry. For example, job seekers who want to work in finance typically search only for jobs in investment banking. While pretty much every large corporation has a financial analyst position, Wessel advises that by broadening your search, you will be surprised how well your skills and interests may match a job you might never have considered.

2. Be flexible

Liz's next tip is to remain open to relocating to where your best job opportunity is. She notes that some of the optimal "starter cities" are in the Midwest. New York City, Chicago, or Los Angeles are not going to be the perfect fit for everyone.

She goes on to explain that relocating can be a useful tool for growth, an opportunity to learn more about oneself and to develop independence. If you move somewhere strictly because you have friends or family there, you just might miss out on an ideal opportunity. Besides, allowing yourself to get too comfortable can kill a career in no time flat.

3. "REAF" for the skies

When it comes to landing a job or internship, Wessel recommends that job seekers use the REAF Method. REAF, an acronym created by WayUp, is a four-step method that breaks down as follows:

Research: Search for three facts about the company, those surprises that even the interviewer is unaware of. By showing your "insider knowledge" of the company upfront, you're sure to make an excellent first impression.

Also, look for company employee profiles on LinkedIn or Twitter with similar job roles as yours. This research will help you understand your job duties and bring more to the interview table. Lastly, research who'll be interviewing you. Determine if you both share some common interests. This will help you connect more effectively with them, making the conversation more meaningful and flowing more naturally.

Enthusiasm: The last thing an interviewer wants is to meet with a person who seems gloomy and uninterested in the interview process. Your confidence and enthusiasm reflect your personality. Your posture and body language should convey that you are engaged in the interview and that your attention is focused. To show your enthusiasm, Liz suggests using comments such as, "I'm so excited to meet you!" and "Thanks so much for taking time to speak with me!"

Ask Questions: Liz suggests preparing at least three questions to ask at the end of the interview. These questions should center on the company's values, expectations for its employees, its current priorities, and related topics.

Follow-up: Liz recommends that you follow up with your interviewers and recruiters via email within twelve hours of the interview, thanking them for their time. However, you shouldn't assume you'll hear back immediately after your follow-up. Based on her experience at Google, Liz noted that offers were not made until two to three months after the interview, and that a full five months passed before the offer arrived after she initially submitted her application.

However, if your interviewer indicates that you'll hear back by the end of April and you haven't received any updates by May 1st, you may send a brief note inquiring about the status of your application.

Following these tips can help you nail an interview and lock down that all-important job. They will demonstrate that you are prepared and interested, and will go a long way in helping you stand out from the competition.

Founder Resistance–the Art of Managing Up

I believe we are all founders—founders of our future, careers, and businesses.

Managing up is very different from "managing down" or "managing your peers." But you are not alone in this, so do not hesitate.

Let's look deeper into the fine art of managing up, a technique that will help you overcome founder resistance:

It's not about trenching in or convincing others of your position. It's about playing an active role in the picture and managing relationships more effectively.

Your boss or superior can't be at all places at all times. You should be able to find and present the solution to your boss by using:

The C-Suite Decision Formula

- What is the cost?
- What is the benefit?

- What is the risk?
- What is the reward?

When you present an idea to your boss, present it in the way that:

- Mitigates the risk
- Shines a spotlight on the benefits
- Eases their anxiety

Other questions to ask include: "What if we don't do this?" You are navigating a tricky relationship as you are 'managing up.' It's different from directing a subordinate. You must explain to them why. They hesitate because they are not as close to your achievable issues. Your superior is blocked, and you need to help unblock him. Make it easier for them. Give them the benefits, the costs, the risks, and the rewards.

This is a simple yet effective decision-making formula that you can use to demonstrate your competence and influence within your space.

A case study on successfully 'managing up.'

Where does it all fit? The natural laws of each season help us overcome obstacles in our lives, in our jobs, and in our everyday lives. But how exactly? Let me walk you through the story of Jill, who used 'managing up' to overcome her obstacles and succeed.

At some point in her life, Jill took on a huge job–Chief Administrative Officer to the CEO. She is a very competent person. But soon after she assumed her responsibilities, the CEO, Alan, came to me and said, "I don't know if this is going to work out." I met with Jill and asked her, "How are you feeling? How is it sitting?" She just burst into tears and said, "I don't know if this is going to work."

I took a moment to reflect. I told her, "Oh, I know what we have to do. We will get through this. First, let's see what your strengths are. You're doing a fantastic job of working with your peers; all of them love you, and you love them. You're doing a fantastic job of delegating, and you're a great fit here. Everybody loves you. What's eating you alive is the CEO, who desperately needs you. You need to find a way to manage him. You need to manage up."

She said, "How am I going to do that?"

I said, "With the 'This or That' game. Imagine you have some buckets. At your work, you have your dailies, weeklies, monthlies, and quarterlies. That's the stuff you must always do. So that's your "Must Do" bucket. There are also training and development paths within this category. Special projects, strategic initiatives.

Then there are the occasions when the CEO just flies in and barks a bunch of urgent, top-priority demands at you. You have to do those. Then, in addition to that, there's some personal work that Alan is asking you to do. There may even be more buckets. But you have only so many hours in a day."

Then I told her a story. "Now imagine you're at the bottom of a grain elevator in the middle of Manitoba. This is your new job: trucks are going to come and throw grain down at you. Take the shovel and spread it around so it's evenly distributed. I leave and close the door behind me. You're in the silo. Five trucks, then 10 trucks come. The grain is now reaching up to your knees, and you're like, 'I'm not sure if I can do this,' but you keep shoveling. The trucks just keep coming. Now the grain is above your waist.

What should you do? Should you just keep shoveling, or should you raise the alarm to me, the boss, and say, 'Susan, I see an emerging issue. I'm not drowning yet, but I am concerned that if these trucks keep coming at this rate, I'm not going to be able to get on top of this. I'm not going to be able to spread this grain out. I'm afraid it's going to get above my mouth, and I'll drown.'

It is your responsibility to tell me this; that there are emerging issues. It's also your responsibility to give me some suggestions or solutions. You're the closest one to this. You can say, 'Susan, you can slow the trucks down, so I can keep up and climb on top, or you get me somebody to shovel with and we'll handle it. But if we keep up like this, I'm going to suffocate.'

"I'm your boss. It's your responsibility to also manage me, to manage up. You do it respectfully. This is what's called management. Management isn't just taking a list of tasks and running through them. It's a collaborative exercise where you have to raise the alarm and say, "I see an emerging issue. We're not going to hit our goal. We're running out of money. We need more resources on it."

I told Jill, "You need to do that with Alan, but in a really respectful way, and you've got to be able to figure out what you can do in the first place."

In addition to the Must Do bucket, here are a few other buckets you may want to implement:

- Share Bucket
- Care Bucket
- Trash Bucket

You can always create additional buckets according to your needs.

So we played the 'This or That' game together. I said, "I want you to take all of the buckets, put everything in those buckets that you know you have to do or that has been asked of you to do. Then we will conduct a grouping exercise in which we assign time blocks to groups. We'll assess the level of effort required for these.

Then we're going to sit down with Alan, and you're going to share it with him and ask, 'Is it this or is it that? I can do the training, but I can't do it this week. If I complete the training, it will take eight days to obtain my certification, which means I will be out of the office for eight days. Are you okay with that? If I do go for eight days, do you want me to bring somebody in to cover, or do you want me to just leave it? It's this or that."

In Jill's case, the This or That game focused on developing a work plan with respectful boundaries, including daily, weekly, monthly, quarterly, and annual guidelines, and on creating time and space for special projects and strategic initiatives as they arise. We want to focus on our regular work approximately two-thirds of the time and be strategic at least during the remaining one-third. The Golden Circle rule works beautifully here.

She did that the next weekend, and she felt great. On Monday, she presented it to her boss, and he loved it. This new approach worked beautifully for Jill and Alan.

Community

> "Spring is nature's way of saying, 'Let's party!'"
>
> — ROBIN WILLIAMS

The Spring season is characterized by a sense of newness and freshness as the earth gradually shakes off the cold. Tender shoots emerge from the earth and tiny leaves unfurl from barren trees. There is a sense of hope and celebration. The soft greens of foliage and rainbow hues of spring flowers bring color back to the world.

Reconnecting with those we lost touch with over the cold months is natural during this phase. It's a time for catching up. The season inspires both starting new relationships and nurturing the ones we already have. Communities begin to come together regularly through programs, activities, and events.

Here are just a few cultural celebrations that take place in the Spring:

- India's Spring Festival
- Easter
- Nowruz, which commemorates the first day of Spring, usually falls on March 21. It is celebrated as the beginning of the New Year by over 300 million people worldwide, and has taken place for over 3,000 years in the Middle East, the Balkans, Central Asia, the Black Sea Basin, and more.[5]
- Cinco de Mayo
- Spring Equinox at Chichen Itza and Teotihuacan pyramids in Mexico
- Stonehenge Spring Equinox Celebration[6]
- Shunbun No Hi (Spring Equinox in Japan)
- Cimburijada in Zenica, Bosnia

There are many others. Spring is a natural time of celebration, and it is widely celebrated worldwide.

5. United Nations Website. "International Nowruz Day: 21 March." UN.org. Accessed June 16, 2022. https://www.un.org/en/observances/international-nowruz-day

6. Lyons, Thomas. "Stonehenge, Sacrilege and the spirit of spring equinox." The Spaces. Accessed June 16, 2022. https://thespaces.com/stonehenge-sacrilege/

Birds and other animals migrate in the Spring. Climate change has definitely caused a shift in the transition from winter to spring. Winter becomes shorter, Spring occurs sooner, Summer lasts longer, and Fall arrives later.

In your community, here are some ideas you can try to create "Spring Catch Up":

- Organize a block party or common-use-area neighborhood party (at a local park, for example).
- Invite people to create brief, newsy emails to send out to the community to let them know what their family has been up to during the fall and winter, and to announce upcoming spring events that they can invite neighbors to attend.
- Consult your local city hall or government offices for guidelines on disposing of materials that the recycling center may not accept, such as potentially hazardous materials like old paint cans, obsolete computers and their accessories, and other items for which disposal is unclear.

Once you have the guidelines, organize a "Pick-up" day where a truck will collect those items and transport them so they can be disposed of legally and properly.

Natural Laws of Spring

Rebirth

Themes of rebirth and renewal often use symbols associated with Spring. Thoughts and emotions of love, hope, and youth also fill the season. We are moving towards Easter and the coming of the light. It's time to reassess our actions and set our sights on new beginnings and new vistas.

Balance

The spring equinox is about finding that balance between light and darkness, between life and death. The same applies to your life and work—it's about finding the right time for everything and balancing your priorities. An animal that is attuned to nature won't waste its time sunbathing when what it needs is food. Nor will it hunt when it's time to build a nest. The law of survival dictates our priorities. It dictates balance.

Awakening

Spring is a time of awakening. Plants, animals, and water – everything becomes alert and awake. There's much to learn from this and much to gain from allowing this natural sequence to influence our lives. Now is the time to reset and rejoice. The things that don't look right or that don't fit our notions are easily noticeable during this time. Get moving and clean out all of the dirt and dust. Out with the old, in with the new.

Exploration

As the flora and fauna shed their winter habits, they begin to explore. There is no better way to pass the season for us as well —nothing better than to run and explore at this time. To find new ways out of old habitats and to rejoice in our ingenuity.

Spring Business Ideas and Activities

Earth Day occurs on April 23rd of every year, after all, and it's the perfect way to celebrate spring! This season is also an ideal time to engage your employees and community in activities that exemplify renewal, purging the old, and welcoming the new. Not everything you implement needs to involve sales or business growth, however. Spring is an ideal time of year to host outdoor events that engage your community. Some ideas include:

- Planting trees, flowers, or bushes in high-use community areas like parks or building neighborhood communal gardens
- Scheduling a day to pick up litter and trash around the community and on local roads and highways
- Hosting a local picnic and/or nature walk and inviting community members.
- There are numerous ways in which your business can contribute to enriching your community while engaging residents in fun, enriching activities. Doing so helps build goodwill and establishes your company as a community-minded and involved entity.

Natural Law and Jill's case

The idea of 'managing up' is based on a fundamental natural law. Seasons and natural law tie together. I directed Jill to that specific law, prioritizing survival. What is a spring bear like? For example, a fall bear is gaining weight and preparing for hibernation. A winter bear is in their den. They're hibernating. Everything slows down. A spring bear is starving and running to get some food. It comes down to this:

There's a right time for everything.

Here's another example. When a tree is growing, it's growing–it's not hibernating at the same time. There's a time and a place for everything, but you have to structure it, and you've got to organize it. You have to anchor it and tie it down to core priorities.

Jill worked feverishly. What she needed was a structure, so I directed her to the 'buckets' idea and the natural cadence of that work. It really worked for her. She came up with the 'Daily Fly In' bucket, where Alan would fly in with something and drop it on her lap, such as scheduling meetings, last-minute travel, and creating meeting reminders for him. Then there was the training and development, which came after the 'Must-Do' bucket.

When you look at birds, the mama bird has to feed her kids. Then in her spare time, she might splash around in the bird-bath. It's a matter of survival, coupled with the quality of life. Alan doesn't want her running around looking like her head is going to pop off her shoulders. Jill and anyone else in a similar role to hers must project that they have everything well in hand, but there also needs to be enough 'me, myself, and I' time.

You are not a bad person. You are the best of the best. You are the best person for this job, but you must educate your supervisor. You need to impose the idea that there is a time and a place for everything. Trust the process. Establish the structure and respect the natural law. If we blow you up, put you through the washing machine, and spit you out, we failed. You failed, too, though, because you didn't manage this structure. Architect a process and ensure that boundaries are set.

Jill was a brand new person after this coaching session. She put it all together, and she's relieved. Now you put capacity into it. Now you see the cadence. You see what happens at a particular time in a specific rhythm. Winning together. Communication, respect boundaries. Success.

Jill became the hero in her own story. Furthermore, she

supported Alan more effectively, allowing him to be the hero in his story.

Leadership Lesson for Spring

> The day the Lord created hope was probably the same day he created Spring.
>
> — BERNARD WILLIAMS (ENGLISH PHILOSOPHER)

Even when you feel that all hope is lost, Spring brings with it the vibration of hope and renewal. Leaders and adult role models need to plug into that amazing energy and spread hope and encouragement. Here's a fantastic lesson that I received about this out of the mouth of babes, in this case, from my son Robbie:

Be Present

My world shattered when my husband left. For three years, I cried constantly, especially during car rides with my young sons, Robbie and Cash. I thought I was hiding it well, but children are perceptive.

One day, Robbie's innocent question pierced through my fog of grief: "Mommy, do you think today could be a happy day?" When I tried to deflect, he went on an impassioned rant about the difference between happy and sad days. His words hit me hard:

"Mommy, this is what a happy day looks like. Everyone is smiling; they're jumping around; they're excited. Sometimes people are hugging each other. That's a happy day. On sad days, people hunch their shoulders. Mom, every day has been a sad day for a long, long time."

I tried to reassure him that things would improve someday, but he challenged me: “Mom, I am sick of your somedays. Can today be a happy day?”

This moment was a wake-up call. I realized that my constant sorrow was affecting my children more than I’d imagined. I made a conscious decision to change, understanding that “Your face should light up when you see your kids, period.”

This experience taught me the importance of being present and directing emotions appropriately. I learned to greet people with genuine warmth and engagement, whether at home or in the workplace. By focusing on the moment and the people in front of me, I found that everything changed. This shift in perspective not only improved my relationships with my children but also enhanced my interactions in all aspects of life. Being present became my new way of navigating the world, allowing me to connect more authentically with others and find joy in daily interactions.

The Power of Connectivity: The Bus Route Case Study

When I moved to Swift Current, Canada, I became the person responsible for running the city. I had considerable authority to make decisions and implement changes. One day, I noticed that people who used the food bank had difficulty getting home with their food because there was no reliable bus system. The problem with the bus system made me realize that many people in our community struggled to get around easily, which made it difficult for them to work, attend school, or access food.

I assembled a team to create a regular bus route to help everyone in the community. It wasn’t easy. Many people didn’t want it. Some people said it would bring “unwanted” people to town.

Some people said it would be too expensive. Some people said it could not be done.

But I knew that all parts of a community working together are essential. Just like all the layers in a painting. We need everyone to be supported and included for economic prosperity.

After a lot of hard work, we were finally able to start the bus route. It benefited the entire community, not just the bus riders. Workers could get to their jobs, older adults could get around, and businesses got more customers. The bus connected all the different parts of our community.

Advice for you:

1. Look around your community and try to spot problems that others might not see.
2. Remember that helping one group of people often benefits everyone.
3. Don't give up when people disagree with your ideas. Build a business case. Also, listen actively and learn more about concerns. Ask questions; collaboration will yield a solution that works. Don't push too hard. Don't pull too hard. Find the middle ground. Remember to facilitate lasting change, a champion is required. Be the change you wish to see in the world. Lean on courageous leadership.
4. Think about how all the different parts of your community work together, like layers in a painting.
5. Focusing on small changes, such as a bus route, can make a big difference in many people's lives.
6. When you grow up, use your power and influence to help others and make your community better for everyone.

Bus Route Lesson

Be fully present and intentional in your interactions. Your genuine emotional state and focus can significantly affect relationships and outcomes in both personal and professional settings. By consciously directing your emotions and attention to the person you're interacting with, you create more meaningful connections and avoid misdirecting unrelated feelings onto others. Be open and be creative. Workshop together with an open mind.

Inclusivity and loneliness

Takeaway:

Creating inclusive communities can help combat loneliness by ensuring no one feels left out or ignored. Connection: Just as designing the bus service can help everyone, community initiatives to reduce loneliness should cater to diverse groups - young, old, newcomers, long-time residents, and others.

Layers of community and social connections:

Recognizing the various "layers" in a community can help identify isolated individuals and create targeted strategies to integrate them. Connection: Different social groups (e.g., retirees, young professionals, families) may experience loneliness in distinct ways. Addressing the unique needs of each layer can create a more connected community overall.

Overcoming misconceptions about loneliness:

Like the misconceptions about the bus service, there are often misunderstandings about loneliness and its solutions. Connection: Educating the community about the prevalence and impact of loneliness can foster empathy and motivate collective action to address it.

Connectivity as an antidote to loneliness:

Just as the bus connected different parts of the community, creating opportunities for social connection can help combat loneliness. Connection: Implementing "social connectors" – events, spaces, or programs that bring people together – can be as impactful as physical connectors such as bus routes.

Multiple beneficiaries in addressing loneliness:

Efforts to reduce loneliness can have wide-ranging benefits beyond the immediate targets. Connection: Designed to reduce loneliness and improve overall community well-being, mental health, and even economic productivity.

Diverse needs in social connection

Connection:

Recognize that people have different social needs and preferences. Connection provides various social opportunities, from major community events to smaller, more intimate gatherings, catering to different comfort levels and interests.

Tangible results in reducing loneliness:

Implement measurable initiatives and celebrate visible progress. Connection: Set concrete goals for reducing loneliness (e.g., increasing social participation rates) and publicly acknowledge achievements to maintain momentum.

Economic impact of addressing loneliness:

Recognize the economic benefits of a socially connected community. Connection: Reducing loneliness can lead to improved mental health, increased productivity, and reduced healthcare costs, benefiting the entire community economically.

Holistic thinking about social connection:

Address loneliness as part of a larger community wellness strategy. Connection: Integrate loneliness prevention into various aspects of community planning - from urban design to public health initiatives.

Pride in community action against loneliness:

Foster a sense of collective achievement in creating a more connected community. Connection: Encourage community members to take ownership of anti-loneliness initiatives and to celebrate their roles in fostering a more socially connected environment.

Additional Lessons

Clean–clean your house, your thoughts, your business. Out with the old, in with the new.

Sow–plant your future and move ahead with your plans.

Build–while seasons come and go, some things are made to last. Build your bases during spring, and come back to them every year.

Leadership Snack Pack

CHECK yourself before you WRECK yourself.

Name it to claim it.

Take a close look at yourself. Exercise self-awareness. Are you presenting executive presence? Are you putting your best foot forward?

Name it.

Claim it.

Try and improve.

Conclusion – Spring: The Season of Beginnings

Spring marks the fresh start of your leadership journey, the season when new ideas break through, energy rises, and you feel the pull toward growth. This is your invitation to plant intentionally, to choose with purpose, and to prepare for the momentum ahead. Instead of filling in the answers for you, this chapter asks you to step fully into the role of author and architect of your own renewal.

As you close this spring chapter, take a moment to reflect:

Who Is in Your Spring Circle?

Who are the five to ten people you *want* beside you as you begin again?

Who energizes you, challenges you, supports you, and widens your vision?

What Activities Will You Do?

What practices will help you stretch, awaken, and build momentum?

What routines or rituals will nourish your creativity, clarity, and courage?

Where Will You Do Them?

What places make you feel open, focused, or inspired?

Where will your ideas take root?

What Songs Are Playing?

What soundtrack sets the tone for your spring—light, bold, optimistic, or electric?

Which songs stir something in you that feels like possibility?

Top 3 Tasks You Must Accomplish

What three commitments will define your season of beginnings?

What will you plant now that your future self will thank you for?

SUMMER

Lucy Maud Montgomery was a remarkable Canadian author best known for her novels, including *Anne of Green Gables*. She was also a gifted poet. Her beautiful poem *A Summer Day* begins:

> "The dawn laughs out on orient hills
> And dances with the diamond rills;
> The ambrosial wind but faintly stirs
> The silken, beaded gossamers;...

It expresses the essence of a lovely summer's day, and I feel it is a most appropriate beginning for this season's section of the book.

Summer's long, sunny days and warm, balmy nights make it the perfect season for restoration. At this time of year, the sun's heat intensifies, and because we are also part of nature, we are keenly aware of the season's hot qualities. The principles of Ayurveda define this as pitta, the dosha (or bodily humour) made up primarily of fire. Just as the seasons are constantly changing, humans must also adapt to their environment.

During the season of pitta, it's not surprising that our environment reflects the fiery nature of the season. Our restoration time also becomes transformative… vacations, adventures, and outward movement. Social life shifts into a steady state of relaxation with picnics, outdoor concerts, and camping trips.[1]

Introduction to Summer

Summer bursts with growth. The Earth is lush, verdant green and teems with life. Birds sing, squirrels scurry, and the insects and frogs form a noisy, discordant symphony.

Yet there is also an idle aspect to this time of year. At peak hours of the day, it is easy to be lulled into inactivity by oppressive heat and humidity, a weather capable of silencing even the animals. Dreaminess has a way of creeping into our minds under summer's influence as we untether our imaginations.

If Spring correlates with the freshness and enthusiasm of childhood, summer corresponds to the passion and energy of young adulthood. The hot days and warm nights facilitate relaxation and family gatherings. There is a vitality in the heat that makes us feel fierce, purposeful, and adventurous. But like the passion of youth, summer's intensity needs to be tempered to keep from burning oneself out, not only at home, but also at work.

It is a time to work hard and play hard, but also to enjoy and relax. Summer has an outgoing, affable quality that makes it easy to chat with strangers. The conditions encourage socializing and community involvement. Many families make their fondest memories in the summer months. Summer, quite simply, is a time to have fun.

---

1. Banyan Botanicals. "Using Ayurveda to Keep Cool This Summer." Yoga Alliance. June 9, 2017. https://www.yogaalliance.org/About_Yoga/Article_Archive/Using_Ayurveda_to_Keep_Cool_This_Summer

It is the season to rest, relax, restore, stretch, and grow. The intensity of the sun fuels the fire in your belly, generating an abundance of drive and focus. If this push can be moderated with a bit of summertime laziness, business will be invigorated. Naturally growing because all the right ingredients are present.

Summer accelerates and promotes intensified family bonding and community relations. We naturally gravitate towards fun group activities and causes that are near and dear to our hearts.

The Nature of Summer

As the warmest season of the year, Summer temperatures vary based on geographic location. Due to the Earth's curvature and the increased sunlight, areas adjacent to the equator are usually hotter than those close to either the North or South Pole. The polar regions still contain ice, which reflects sunlight.

The summer equinox takes place when the sun is positioned directly over the equator due to the Earth's tilt on its axis. Astronomical Summer occurs on or around June 21st. Then the North Pole is tilted at its maximum toward the Sun; in the Southern Hemisphere, Summer occurs on or around December 22nd, when the South Pole's tilt angle is most sunward.

Summer Solstice falls upon the day when the sun shines for the longest period of time, whereas the equinox takes place when day and night last about the same amount of time.[2]

Animals have developed numerous physiological adaptations that help them remain cool on even the hottest days. For instance, bees lower the temperature in their hives by beating their wings to fan one another and their larvae. Surprisingly, bees

2. Taylor Redd, Nola. "Summer: The Warmest Season." Live Science. March 11, 2022. https://www.livescience.com/24592-summer.html

can also go for a brief swim in the Summer, just a quick dip, to cool down during a hot Summer's day. That's why bird baths often host bees as well as birds in this season. Butterflies also engage in a behavior known as "puddling," where they essentially walk or lightly wade through shallow puddles that are typically muddy. This activity can help them not only cool off, but also collect essential nutrients.

In fact, like humans, most other mammals enjoy swimming. Deer are among many that are excellent swimmers and also love to wade during the height of the summer months.

Cold-blooded reptiles are more prone to overheating than warm-blooded animals because they depend on their environment to regulate body temperature. So to keep cool, lizards, snakes, and other reptiles will often hang out during the heat of the day under logs, burrows they've made or found, near water sources, and under rocks.[3]

The Three-Part Plan for Women's Success: Stop, Start, and Continue

This is what you should start doing if you want to succeed in your career as a woman. You need to name it to claim it. "I did that." "That was me." Say it. Talk often about your contributions. The worst thing you can do is just sit quietly and let people think that others did your work, or that it was someone else's idea.

Women tend not to promote themselves. We tend not to talk about what we've done well or what we've accomplished. The top priority I want you to do right now, so that you can project strength in your career and advance in it, is to: **"Name it to Claim it."**

3. Discovery Place Website. "Ask a Naturalist: How do animals stay cool in the summer?" Discoveryplace.org. Accessed June 21, 2022.

Name all the things you are doing well. Speak frequently about it. Say it like you mean it. Talk often about your contributions. We tend not to do that, and it impedes us.

Next, you need to stop acting like a church mouse. That mentality got me nowhere. My mom would often say, "Just be quiet. Look pretty, work hard, and maybe, just maybe, your boss will notice you. You will get a raise, and you will be fine."

Well, that didn't work at all. Stop acting like a church mouse. Stop sitting there quietly in the corner, tucked away, being unnoticed. That did not work for me at all. I was overlooked, blamed, passed over, and disregarded.

Stop being small. Stop blending in. Stop being like wallpaper. Stop being a church mouse.

Finally, you need to continue being measured for success. Don't overly emote. Check yourself before you wreck yourself. Don't roll your eyes if you don't agree with someone, and don't flush your cheeks if you become upset and frustrated. For God's sake, don't cry. Keep a steady tone. Be measured. Be consistent. Nail a steady cadence. Always speak calmly and consistently; your demeanor should be calm, cool, and collected at all times. If you feel yourself welling up, becoming overwhelmed, or being overly emotional, just step away.

Being successful is being reliable, consistent, measured, and calmly getting across your point.

I know in the early days of my career, I would flush, get hot cheeks, I would eye-roll, and I would cry. I worked very hard on my inner dialogue and self-conversation. The phrase that I would say to myself is, "Check yourself before you wreck yourself."

Another thing you should continue to do is climb the social ladder. Women have nurturing roles at home and often forgo social events associated with work, such as happy hour and golf games. These events are not pleasant to attend. In fact however, they are must attend events where you need to socialize. Why? You will get to know others, and they, in turn, will get to know you, connect more deeply.

By starting to exchange support with others whom you meet, you begin the process of making room to create opportunities for others and, in turn, for others to create opportunities for you. I excluded all social work-related activities from my career early on due to family obligations. Which makes sense, although it made my work and career trajectory more difficult to navigate.

Attend events as often as possible. It's much more important than you might think. As women, we tend to squeeze out any of those extra opportunities. But squeezing out those social events and meetups is a career killer. Continue to network. Focus on creating at least one deep relationship for each event. Activate your network by asking the person with whom you connect whom he or she most admires as a committed, successful networker.

Then ask for just one introduction. Why? In doing so you make it much easier to start to build a strong, supportive network based on quality over quantity. This way, you regularly build one significant opportunity relationship in your network. Ignoring those social engagements and meetups can severely damage your career. Make sure you keep climbing the social ladder, actively networking, forming deep relationships, and leveraging those connections.

My Memories of Summer

Last Supper

My childhood was marked by profound disruption and hardship. When I was in Grade 7, my mother abruptly left our family. Despite living in a "big beautiful house," we were "totally broke" and had suffered neglect and abuse. Her departure was sudden and final:

"Mommy, who's here?" I asked, figuring we had a guest. Maybe it was Grandma from Dauphin. She said, "No one. I'm leaving." "Oh," I said excitedly. "Where are you going?" She answered, "I'm leaving your father."

This event thrust my older sister and me into caretaker roles at a young age, where I cared for five siblings, including a one-year-old. It taught me resilience and resourcefulness in the face of adversity.

Our circumstances deteriorated rapidly after my mother left. We moved to "awful houses in the worst part of town," selling everything of value. This experience showed me how quickly life can change and the importance of adaptability.

Family

Everything starts with our families. It's the space where we set our rhythm, our priorities, which then radiate to the rest of our public lives. Use summer's languid rhythm to set the right tone for your business and the other people in your life.

A Season of Forest Bathing and Grounding

Just as people still bask in sunshine, especially during Summer, one of the things I highly recommend is walking in the woods or under an arbor of trees regularly. This "forest bathing" should be a regular part of your effort to ground yourself in nature. And whenever possible, take your shoes off so your bare feet can connect to the earth. The Earth provides a natural source of electrons through subtle electric fields.

Ground yourself every day if possible. This increases energy in the body and reduces inflammation. You feel better in so many ways. Do this daily during the summer. This was natural for me growing up because I didn't have shoes to wear. Nowadays, I don't wear shoes all summer on purpose, and my kids don't wear shoes, either.

It's an amazing feeling. Kick off your shoes and lose them. Where are my shoes? Who cares? My kids lose their shoes in the Summer and we don't care. We oscillate at a new level and we feel great all summer. We glow.

Set these Summer goals:

- Forest bathe
- Lose your shoes
- Ground yourself
- Meet new people
- Walk in new spaces
- Find your natural rhythm
- Sign new deals for yourself
- At work, sign new deals for others.
- Pay attention to your sleep; sleep better
- Slow down. Trust the process, breathe, relax, and let it grow

Work

To make the most of summer, you have to be sure you are following the rhythm of this season of rejuvenation and connection. It's time to take a small step back, but not completely. Summer is also a time of growth. Use the tools I provide to emerge from this abundant season of fun stronger and wiser.

Summer Burnout and Tipping Points

Despite its fun and relaxing nature, Summer can also bring a sense of being burned out… used up. I'm getting better whenever I go through burnout. I'm not 100% back to normal immediately, but it used to take me three weeks to recover. There's actually a little switch that goes off.

It's like a click. Many people never experience it, but they should. I refer to it as "the unwind." It's when you've unwound and there's this little click, and you go, "Oh, my God. I finally released all of that tension. It's gone."

But it used to take me three to four weeks to get there. When people go on vacation for two weeks, they may never experience it. They don't know what it feels like to be completely recharged.

Find your summer click; people will perform better at work, in life, and at home. They will make better decisions and be more at peace if they can find that space. That is the space of totally recharging for real. But they have to hit that movement of release.

Burnout happens when you never release or you never recharge fully, and you just keep stacking, stacking, stacking, stacking activities, chores, all the different sections of your life until eventually, you're burned out. You're past being overwhelmed. Your resiliency is gone. You lost it.

It's like when a lake dies. There's a tipping point. You can keep throwing poop in the lake. Lots of cities do this. They throw the shit in the river, and the shit ends up in the lake. The lake includes fish, plants, vegetation, rocks, sand, and moving water. It eventually cleans itself. The lake recalculates the balance, except for when it's too much. When it's too much, it actually dies. It depletes the lake of oxygen, and the lake cannot recover. It is on the verge of collapse. Be mindful of the tipping point.

Lake Wilcox in Southern Ontario died. All of these huge, expensive homes were built around this fabulous lake. It was beautiful. Then, one day, the lake died. What happened? It started to rot, so it stank to high heaven. People had to close their windows and couldn't sit in their yards. Their property value plummeted because the lake hit the tipping point. Nobody was paying attention and the lake could not rebound. The oxygen had been choked out of it by sediment - dirt, crap, debris.

Think about a fish tank. You plug it in and it gets oxygenated. You see the bubbles. Now, what happens when you don't oxygenate it? To demonstrate, you could simply put a bowl on the counter and add a couple of fish. After a while, smell it. It starts to rot. Eventually, the oxygen in the water - because of the fish poop and debris - is gone and the water starts to rot and stink.

The natural oxygen in a lake allows the lake to live and thrive. The plants live, the fish live, the fish eat the plants, and the plants continue to thrive and suck up some of the dirt. It's fertilizing the plants, and they're growing and sucking up some of that debris. But when the oxygen is done and the lake's hit a tipping point, all of that stuff settles to the bottom, and it just rots. That's it. Dead lake.

This community had to dredge the lake and shovel all of the shit at the bottom of the lake, get all of the dead fish out of the lake.

These millions of dollars' worth of homes were sitting right beside a rotten, stinking lake.

They consulted all of these scientists. "What do we do? Can we bring the lake back to life?" "No, you can't. The lake is dead." "What?!?" "The lake is dead." You know what they did? They installed a giant "lake lung." It's back, and it doesn't stink anymore and looks vibrant, but it's mechanically supported on Lake Life Support.

This is what people are doing to themselves. They hit a tipping point, and there's just no coming back from it. Now you have to do an intervention because you totally messed up your natural ability to restore. The seasons, as you know, are action and then restoration. Action and then restore. Winter and Summer are times of restoration. In the Summer, it's so important to restore. If you don't, you will reach a tipping point, which we call burnout.

You must be cognizant that this summer is the time to restore. It's there for a reason. It's great to be doing things, but make sure you're also doing the things that are restorative to you. Do them often in the Summer as much as you can.

The work-life blend is gaining traction due to numerous changes in the workplace. The labor construct is shifting to accommodate a more integrated life. They do need boundaries, though. Be sure to embrace the seasonal cadence of activity and restoration.

In Canada, a law was recently enacted that grants workers the right to unplug. It happened because of COVID and people working around the clock. Suddenly, there were no boundaries. There's no, "I'm at home. I'll see you tomorrow. I'll work on it tomorrow." In Canada, they're now saying employees have the right to unplug.

I'm a big advocate of labor choices. I want to work when I want to, the way I want to, and on what I want to. It's the idea that employers should be offering options. As long as outcomes and productivity prosper. Employers can achieve substantially greater outcomes and productivity if they offer a choice model; employers in the traditional model achieve only 50-75% productivity. If you're offering up gig work, flex time or compressed time, you'll get way more out of it in outcomes. It's great for business. It's just not traditional. Your business will prosper. Of course, with a policy like this put into practice must work well for the business regiment.

The Art of Squatting

I'm no stranger to hardship. My experience overcoming those hardships is one of my most prized possessions and has helped me become a strong, intuitive leader.

The 'art of squatting' is one of those experiences that can teach one a lot, if one is listening with eyes and ears wide open. I was homeless for a time as a child and a young adult.

What are the golden rules of a successful squat? Just go to your chosen squatting place, move in, set up shop, and be discreet at night. Don't turn any lights on. Of course, you will not have heat or hot water, absolutely no phone, and some power, albeit limited. Make it your own. Over time, you acquire rights. They are called 'squatter's rights.' If no one kicks you out and, oddly, you have settled in, the place can, in some weird way, become homey.

There is an art to this. It takes some know-how. When I first moved into my squatting place, I was like a complete idiot. I made the fateful mistake of turning the bathroom light on at night, and I almost didn't make it. I remember sleeping on the floor. I remember really being confused and then, over time, learning and perfecting the art of squatting.

The art of squatting is critical for leaders to learn and for people experiencing homelessness. Being a great leader involves understanding. Why do people do what they do when they are desperate? Living in an unused property because you are homeless is a challenge and an art. You have to be creative and smart all at the same time.

On several occasions in my career, I had to deal with people who took over a property, a project, a job, or the like because those who would walk away from it were not owners. Easy to get in, hard to get out. Once they get in, if some time has passed, especially if a long time has passed, they really will have a hard time getting them out. I have encountered this in business many times, and I understand how to handle such situations. This happens with employees taking over jobs that they were not assigned and developers taking over land that was not theirs, and even tenants encroaching, expanding. All of this would have been very challenging to address if I had not learned the art of squatting.

You need to be gentle with these folks. They took more than was theirs, probably because they were desperate, or simply opportunistic. Don't punch down. You will look like an asshole and be crucified for it. Usually, you can't force a squatter out. It requires several steps, finesse, and sometimes substantial funding. Seek legal advice from several sources, and trust your instincts. Be kind. Be firm. Consider your brand. Don't risk erosion.

Do get those squatters out, just do it with grace. This is important for team harmony, market share, your bottom line, and ensuring people on your team work effectively and in harmony.

The Coffee Cup Game

As a leader, ensure that people stay in their lane. Set clear expectations, clear responsibility, and authority. Otherwise, chaos ensues.

Some of the things that I've learned have arisen out of tragedy, or I've known them because of something that went wrong. Like, "What happened to Sears Canada? What happened to Blockbuster Video?" These large companies no longer exist. It's because they missed some of the core principles. They lost sight of these essential pieces. They weren't listening to their team out of arrogance or a lack of consideration. They weren't listening to the guy on the shop floor. Or they missed the telltale signs of squatters moving in on the market share.

Here is a great technique I have used before when I was CAO, and again as CEO. When I was in the boardroom, I would walk around with a coffee cup and listen, watch, and learn. It was like *Undercover Boss* in a way. *Undercover Boss* in plain sight. I not only relied on my direct reports to inform me about what was happening, but I also looked into it myself.

See clearly what is going on. I would verify informally by walking around with a coffee cup. I called it *The Coffee Cup Game*. This works both within the business and with external relationships.

To be sure you don't miss the signs and signals of opportunity and trouble. How do you gain deeper insights into your business and become more innovative? Here are the rules:

- Carry a coffee so it appears you aren't in a hurry.
- Build rapport by poking your head in.
- Ask about their weekend,
- Ask if they need anything

- Ask if there's anything they or you could do differently or better: "Is there any wisdom you can give me?" Or I can share with them. Be curious. Ask questions.
- Meet them where they are and ask for their expertise.
- Shut your mouth and listen more.
- It's the ground game. Front row seats. Look, listen.
- Do you know who really knows? It's the guy on the shop floor—the guy who's been here for 30 years.
- Ask those around you what they would like to change. Change the future. We can't change the past.
- **Action**: Get a coffee, walk around, look, ask & listen.

Why is it that when the people on the street, the workers, the shop floor, the real people, see that you care enough to walk around and do a ride-along, they start to share more openly? I would ask a question now and then, and they would say, "Nobody has ever asked me before." I would ask, "Is there anything that you think we can do differently or better?" That's it. Then I'd shut my mouth. They'd tell me.

I was initially responsible for three different unions and negotiated with them. I closed our union negotiations in record time every single time. Before I arrived, the unions would almost automatically go on strike. Senior management was decimated. The teams were decimated.

For one of the teams I lead that had a Union, we negotiated in half a day because I walked around with a coffee cup, listening to what everybody told me were the issues long before negotiations started. I worked out the problems in advance of the Union negotiations. There were no grievances because I had already addressed all the concerns and a little bit more.

When I sat down to start negotiations, we had already established a really great rapport. We started our discussion with: "Do you guys want to have a pizza party? We can have a pizza party if we get this deal done by noon." That summed up our union negotiations. The agreement was completed in record time, and everyone was satisfied.

The national union head who flew in for the negotiations said he'd never seen anything like it in his life. It was all because of the Coffee Cup Game. Looking, listening, acting in a future-forward, growth mindset. I could meet the workers where they were, because I worked to understand the issues.

Tips – 6 most important things you shouldn't miss out in Summer:

1. Find solutions in the most unusual spaces or moments. Breathe, give space to do nothing
2. Find people who are amazing
3. Connect
4. Build your community, your circle
5. Help others build their community, help others build their circle
6. Find superstars
7. Be intentional about restoring your head, your heart, your health and your home.

I am a superwoman, but I have also come to realize that I have kryptonite that brings me down. I have superpowers, but I also need to be restored and trust the process. I am growing all summer, provided I let it happen.

Early in my career, I ran too fast, burned too brightly, and exhausted myself.

A Season of Promise, Trust, and Growth

You know, when the sun sparkles and dances on the surface of the water, you cannot see where the water ends, and the sky begins to shine. Summer is the season to get some sand between your toes, splash water, and get some Vitamin D into your system.

Pack up, shift gears, and change your environment. Make sure you leave the grind. Step out and walk in new or old spaces. Doesn't matter where. Just go!

Whatever you do in the summer, do not over-jam your schedule. Build in time to let the natural cadence of summer take over. Beach time matters.

The seeds have been sown. Now it's time to leave Mother Nature alone to do her job. You simply lean into summer and let events unfold.

Say 'yes' to tan lines. Say 'no' to worry lines.

I work like crazy leading up to summer, mad dash, run like hell, push hard.

And then…
Release.
Slow down.
Trust the process.
Make room.
Meet new people.
Try new things.
Rest, relax, restore
Grow.

And commit to closing deals in the summer. Deals with yourself, your community, your family, and your work. For example, I made a deal with my son that he can fish off the pier until 10 pm. No matter what. You will connect with people. You will have moments of clarity. The sun is shining brighter, so you can see more clearly. Make space and commit to making things happen when others step away. Do this calmly. Don't overdo it. Trust the space, slow down, and let life catch up. Know that things are growing. Trust Mother Nature. Trust the universe.

How does your garden grow? Make sure you follow these rules for optimal plant growth. Your garden needs *just enough*:

- Sunshine
- Water
- Nutrients
- Light touch

Remember, too much of any one thing and your garden will result in little or no growth. It's the same with people. I'm so grateful to have had the support in my life from my grandfather, my grandmother, my sisters, my brothers, my father, my mother, and, in general, my ancestors. I have been given so much and yet not enough, but with the right amount of water, light, and nutrients, I am bursting out.

In my childhood, I never, ever had enough, yet those hard lessons allowed me to navigate adulthood and leadership with the wisdom given to me by generations of leadership.

I am growing exponentially now because I am ready.

Ensure that you build, maintain, and activate your summer circle.

Trust the process. Summer shows us that everything happens when it is meant to happen. Just lean back and trust that, just as

Summer shows us the bounty of her gifts of nature, your efforts will show you that you will benefit from the hard work, leadership, and relationships you cultivate. Your outcomes are not by accident. Leverage your network. Build your network. Activate your network.

Summer's promise is real. Release and open up to great things!

> "One must maintain a little bit of summer, even in the middle of winter."
>
> — HENRY DAVID THOREAU

HR is a sales function.

Summer is a time for growth, and this often means hiring new people. When bringing new recruits into your work community, you must ensure you focus on what really matters.

What do these people want? They want to win. This is a game of natural law. They want to feel that, if they join this company, they will be successful. It's not only about what *you* want, more so "*Can* they do the job?" It's also about "*Will* they do the job?" Are they going to win if they join your team? Can they? Will they?

Say you want to hire a Director of Marketing. You've got the fish on the hook, but then you pull and the line breaks. Why? Because you pulled too hard at the wrong time. You didn't use a strong enough line. What should the line have been?

You recruit to see if they can do the job. Once you are satisfied that they can do the job, you offer them the job. But you only do 50% of the work in bringing them on. If you continue to lose potential personnel, you will likely stop at 50% every time.

Once you are satisfied that they can do the job, you move too fast and scare them away. They shut down because they're unsure whether they can succeed. Will they be impactful? Will the job line up with their lifestyle? Will this satisfy their work and life needs? What's in it for them? What's in it for you? How long is their commute? Are you okay with hybrid work until they contribute huge?

After an executive leader lost another preferred candidate recruit for a Key role he was desperate to fill, I asked him, "Did you talk to this potential candidate about our leadership development and training opportunities?" He said, "No, that never came up." "Did you ask them where they lived and how far of a commute it would be? Did you tell them that we would be flexible on a hybrid work arrangement?"

He replied, "I have to drive into work. It's only a 45-minute commute." I said, "Okay, does he have kids?" "Yes, he has two kids." 'Okay, well that's probably why he didn't take the job." He said, "That didn't come up." Who will take his kids to school? Does his wife or family have time to do school pickup and drop-off?

This is my point. He proved that he can do the job on Friday. You offered him the job on Friday. He talked it over with his wife over the weekend and talked about if this would actually fit into their lives, how it would fit, and if he would be impactful and successful. They concluded on Monday morning that it wouldn't work for their family because you forgot about the other 50%.

It's a natural law. They can do the job, but will they? Why would they? People lean in when they think that they're going to be successful at something.

Sprint for Success

Summer is the fastest and easiest period for growth. Be intentional about growing naturally, and with abundance in mind. Everyone can do it with the right ingredients. This is because nobody else is doing that. That's when they go on their summer breaks. Think about it this way: every army that has attempted to march itself through Winter has lost the war. Napoleon lost to the Russians, as did the Germans. But if you start to follow those rhythms in Summer, you stand the best chance of success. The sun is shiny, sprinkles of rain, heat, and repeat.

When everybody was half asleep this summer, I signed four new clients. My boss asked, "How did you do that?" It's because people are on vacation, and their kids aren't in school. They're not driving all over the place, and guess what happens? They want to speak with me for an hour. Try to book an owner or founder's time in the fall. You can't get them.

I'd have great calls with these guys. I'd ask, "Where are you right now?" They'd say, "I'm just driving out to my cottage. I've got at least two hours to talk." I'll take it. We have a completely different call than if I had booked him through his secretary, and he fits me in amongst 50,000 other things.

Summer is a time to slow down and speed up. A time for growth, if you dial into summer right. At the right time, and the right place.

Community

Summer is the perfect time to connect with your community. Everyone is out and about, enjoying the outdoors, open to invitations and to other people. Use the season wisely, and foster new or strengthen existing ties. You will need a strong community when you enter fall. And an even stronger one, come winter.

Evaluate your circle. Reflect, renew, and conduct an empty-chair exercise. Identify who should join your circle for optimal success and strength.

Modern-Day Summer Traditions Around the World

We've just explored some of the ancient traditions of Summer. Here are a few that are still celebrated today.

In Russia, White Nights are celebrated in St. Petersburg in June. This is a time of year when complete nightfall doesn't take place. It tends to become a sun-drunk festival which includes concerts and various forms of celebration.

The city of Fairbanks, Alaska, experiences continuous daylight for several periods during the Summer, and since 1906, the Midnight Sun baseball game has been held there.

Guatemala and other countries that form the cradle of the ancient Mayan Civilization mark the Summer Solstice with spiritual rituals at sunrise and sunset at various Mayan ruins.

Japan holds the Aomori Nebuta Matsuri Festival, a beautiful parade of lantern floats, some of which take up to a year to create. These feature sculptures and depictions of famous pop culture characters, gods, and historic figures. Another popular Summer tradition there is the Sumidagawa Fireworks Festival.

During midsummer in Spain, bonfires and fireworks are popular forms of celebration. Perhaps the most famous event in that country at this time of year, though, is the town of Bunol's famous La Tomatina, where tens of thousands of people engage in food fights with tomatoes![4]

There are many other Summer celebrations worldwide. I encourage you to take part in activities and events that you thoroughly enjoy, which represent this lovely season's amazing features!

Identify a community activity, attend regularly, participate, be intentional. This breaks the downward trend of loneliness.

Vacations

> A vacation is having nothing to do and all day to do it in.
>
> — ROBERT ORBEN

In the Western World in particular, Summer vacations were a staple, an eagerly anticipated time of year for many decades. However, in contemporary culture, the reinvigorating recharge provided by those vacations has largely disappeared. This has caused an unnatural halt to the flow of Summer for many, and adopting an "all work, no play" mindset that eliminates vacations takes a toll not only on the individual but also on everyone around them.

Case in Point: In 2020, 72% of Americans didn't take a Summer vacation, and 44% of working Americans didn't use any of their PTO (paid time off) during Summer. To top it off, another 22% took less time off than normal.[5] While much of this can be attributed to the pandemic and quarantine, travel lockdowns, and more, this could definitely mark the beginning of an

4. Ibid.
5. Holmes, Tamara E. "72% of Americans Did Not Take a Summer Vacation This Year." Value Penguin. September 2, 2020. https://www.valuepenguin.com/travel/americans-did-not-take-summer-vacation

unhealthy pattern that potentially creates overwhelm, maximum stress, and physical, mental, and emotional overload. Vacations are necessary for one's well-being and life balance.

Whether you go out of town or create a fun staycation, I urge you to make time in your schedule for a Summer break, even if it's just for 3 days or a week. It's vital for staying balanced, energized, highly creative and for your peace of mind.

The Summer Paradox: Embracing Growth Amidst the Heat

As the sun climbs higher in the sky and the days stretch longer, we find ourselves in the heart of summer – a season that paradoxically offers both opportunity and challenge. The warmth that coaxes flowers from the earth and fruit from the vine can also wilt our spirits and drain our energy. Yet, within this crucible of heat and humidity lies a unique chance for personal growth and renewal.

The Mid-Year Crossroads

Summer, perched at the year's midpoint, naturally invites reflection. We stand at a crossroads, looking back at the path we've traveled and forward to the road ahead. For many, this reflection can elicit unease. Have we accomplished enough? Are we where we thought we'd be? This introspection, while valuable, can sometimes lead to what psychologists call "imposter syndrome" – a nagging doubt about our abilities and achievements.

But consider this: the very act of questioning is a sign of growth. It shows that you care deeply about your journey and have the courage to examine it honestly. Rather than letting these thoughts overwhelm you, use them as fuel for the fire of your ambition.

Balancing Act: Work, Play, and Recovery

The summer months often bring an influx of social engagements and a surge in workload as colleagues take vacations. While this can be exhilarating, it also presents a challenge: how do we balance our professional responsibilities with the siren call of summer fun?

The key lies not in grand gestures or herculean efforts but in small, consistent acts of self-care. Research has shown that the benefits of a vacation can fade within days of returning to work. Instead of relying solely on these larger breaks, cultivate a practice of daily renewal. Step outside for a brief walk during your lunch break, feeling the warmth of the sun on your skin. Take a moment to meditate, even if it's just for five minutes between meetings. These small acts of mindfulness can act as a balm for your spirit, helping you navigate the increased demands of the season.

Harnessing Summer's Creative Potential

Interestingly, Harvard researchers have found that warmer months can boost creativity, even as they make routine tasks more challenging. This presents an opportunity: use the summer's energy to tackle projects that require innovative thinking or to brainstorm new ideas for the coming months. Save more administrative tasks for cooler parts of the day when your mind might be sharper for detail-oriented work.

The Road Ahead

As you navigate the summer months, remember that burnout is not an inevitable destination. It's a signpost alerting you to the need for change. Unlike depression, which the World Health

Organization classifies as a mental health condition, burnout is described as an "occupational phenomenon." This means it's tied to our work and life circumstances – factors we often have the power to influence.

So, as the heat of summer intensifies, let it serve as a reminder to tend to your inner fire. Nurture it with small, consistent acts of self-care. Feed it with creativity and reflection. And remember, just as summer eventually gives way to the cooler winds of autumn, this challenging period too shall pass. You have the strength within you not only to endure but also to thrive.

The path forward isn't about pushing harder or working longer hours. It's about working smarter, caring for yourself more deliberately, and recognizing that true productivity comes from a place of balance and inner peace. As you move through these warm months, carry with you the knowledge that you are growing, learning, and becoming more resilient with each passing day. Take time to find your summer circle. Connect deeply with them every summer. For example, I have Ladies Movie Nights at Clubhouse Beach. Same beach, same ladies, different movies. This simple event grounds me and gives me a sense of peace and belonging.

Your journey is uniquely yours. Embrace it, challenges and all, and watch as you blossom in ways you never thought possible.

The Nuance

When my son Robbie was 15, I had a fight with him. He was doing online school. He should have been halfway through grade 10 and is not supposed to start grade 11 until the fall. I learned that he has almost finished grade 11. He was speeding through these online courses, getting straight As. But he sped through the courses so that he could play video games all day. The child is sleeping in; he won't go to school; he's up all night. He's killing me.

I opened my big trap and said to him, "Every person in this house needs to either go to school or get a job. He's like, "Fine. I'll get a job." I said, "You're not getting a freaking job. What are you talking about?" He said, "I'll get a job and I'll keep doing these courses just to get school out of the way because school is a complete inconvenience." I'm like, "Alright. Go get a job." Boom.

He went to the leading IT startup campus, where the top IT companies operate out of a large building called Catalyst. He asked them if he could be an intern. Robbie has heard me talk about Zach, who was one of my interns. So he understands internships. Notably, Robbie obtains an internship at a media company and offers to work there for free.

Because he immersed himself in the city's top IT talent, success and opportunity began to come his way. The greatest opportunities have come this way. He's like a goldfish. He's reaching up to what is around him; he's become who he's walking with; he's walking with people and standing near them, and he becomes one of them.

He chose to stand near abundance and success, and hung out there until some of it splashed onto him. He didn't concern himself with looking like a loser. He entered there without arrogance and offered to be helpful.

Then, everyone was asking me, "Can you help my son?" Yes, I would ask around. Hang out where you want to be. Be meaningful. Zach is the son of one of my friends. That's why I took Zach on. Anything he'll do for me is far better than nothing. Zach was learning, and I was benefiting too.

People get stuck with excuses for why they wouldn't ask, why they wouldn't offer something, or why they wouldn't go and stand near it. Ask for an internship. You've got to put all of the excuses aside. Go stand where you want to be. Be where you want to be. Immerse yourself in it in whatever way. Even if that means you're mopping the floor. It doesn't matter. Go walk with the people you want to walk with. Connect and talk with a community you want to be a part of. Show up. Contribute.

There's a little nuance there. It's the butterfly effect. One small thing leads to another small thing, which leads to another small thing. The same is true if you hang out where the gangs hang out or where the crime hangs out. That too will pull you in. One little thing will lead to the next, and the next thing you know, you're a criminal. Or, a person with ideas, but with high-performance smart people striving for excellence. You are who you walk with.

That's what I did when I went to the University of Waterloo. I was punching way above my weight. I went all the way to the University of Waterloo and said, "I want to be here." One little thing led to another little thing. People helped me. They opened the door. I just leaned in. Robbie did that at Catalyst. He leaned in. Zach is doing that with me. They both leaned in.

I look at all the excuses and the people who ask, "How do you do it?" Insert yourself into their community. Just be there. Ask for help. Ask to be invited. Eventually, you will make it. It's not about the fear of failure as much as it is about looking like a loser. That stops people from trying. Find a circle. Stand nearby. Ask to join. Contribute.

Go where the opportunity is. This brings me to my next point:

Immersion by proximity

So many people get mired down with "reasons" (Translation: Excuses). But how do you explain people who are able to accomplish everything they intend to accomplish? Who attains the goals they set for each season in spite of all setbacks? How did they do that? I learned a lot by watching Oprah and reading as many books as I could. This might sound silly, but it worked for me. You've got to go stand by in abundance. When I went to the University of Waterloo, I stood near other successful people.

Go stand or sit near them.

When I went to Waterloo, people were generous to me. They saw me. If they didn't see me, they wouldn't have helped me. Pretend I stayed in rural Manitoba; the University of Waterloo would never know who I was. Go where the abundant people are. Look for the invitations. Schools have them. Chambers of commerce have them. Find a circle where you want to be. Connect.

When you start, be a *passionate learner*. I've always loved people who wanted to understand their biography—where did you come from? I would always wonder, "How did all these people get here?" I was incredibly curious about people. What attributes of a community in a person do you admire? What do you see as success? Go find your circle. Ask to join.

Protect Your Community: Challenge Up on Ethics and Integrity

Never remain silent on ethics violations.

Enron, WorldCom, and other organizations show how ethics violations can damage or destroy even the most valuable companies.

If your management ever asks you to do anything that violates corporate ethics, refuse. Don't do it, and immediately let upper management know of your concerns.

Operate with high integrity.

Such actions ultimately benefit your company, customers, co-workers, and yourself.

Do not assume that management has intentionally requested that you do something wrong when challenging up.

In some cases, inappropriate requests may arise from misunderstandings or poor communication.

Try to present your case in a manner intended to be helpful, not judgmental.

Remember, you have friends: Integrity, consistency, and perseverance.

Action: Monitor for ethics violations in your personal community. Always act with high integrity to protect and pursue your spot in the circle. If the circle stinks, leave and find a better circle.

Natural Laws for Summer

Summer often lulls us into a relaxed state, but it's crucial to recognize and seize the unique opportunities it presents. Instead of passively participating in a routine, boring staff meeting, take the initiative to transform it. When it's your turn to report, engage your colleagues by presenting a problem you're facing and requesting their input. Invite them to a collaborative lunch the next day to discuss solutions. This simple act can revitalize team dynamics and foster creativity. The lesson here is twofold:

stay alert to opportunities for positive change, and don't let summer's leisurely pace deter you from taking action.

> "And so with the sunshine and the great bursts of leaves growing on the trees, just as things grow in fast movies, I had that familiar conviction that life was beginning over again with the summer."
>
> — F. SCOTT FITZGERALD, *THE GREAT GATSBY*

Reach Out

Summer is a time for reaching out. You unfurl in the heat of the sun, shooting out into your surrounding environment. It's a matter of survival… the better you know your environment, the farther you reach, the more chances you have to succeed… in life, in family, in work. Seek a circle of community that you admire and respect. The same is true for your work.

Coming Together

Summer is the ideal season to connect. Just as knowing your environment helps you survive, so does building ties and coming together into a vibrant community.

Growth

This is the season of optimal growth. Let your family grow inwardly and outwardly, as well as your work and your community. Allow events to unfold and don't disrupt that natural rhythm. Growth with an intentional and abundant mindset, map it out. Be specific. Ask and you shall receive.

My Seasonal Lesson: How I Broke the Generational Chains

Understanding your position and goals is crucial for seizing opportunities and achieving optimal results. Life transitions, though often seen as disruptive, are inevitable and vital for growth. They offer opportunities to adapt and improve despite their perceived chaos.

To break the intergenerational cycles of poverty, seek a circle of success. Learn about it. Join in any way possible if you can. Show up and consistently contribute. Learn and participate.

Bruce Feiler's book "Life Is in the Transitions: Mastering Change at Any Age" reveals that transitions occur roughly every 12-18 months, with major "lifequakes" happening 3-5 times in a lifetime. A study by Ohio University and University of Arkansas professors found that people often regret inaction during transitions, potentially missing opportunities to avoid negative outcomes.[6]

Short-term regret can motivate corrective action, while long-term regret serves as a reminder to seize opportunities for improvement. This narrative highlights the importance of seizing opportunities and reaching out during life's pivotal moments.

My story begins from a disadvantaged position ("minus one million"), with an absent mother, a neglectful father, and the responsibility of caring for five siblings. However, I came to realize that many successful individuals have overcome similar adversities. Here are a few examples:

- Albert Einstein didn't speak for the first three years of

---

6. Beike, Denise and Markman, Keith. "What We Regret Most Are Lost Opportunities: A Theory of Regret Intensity." ResearchGate. Accessed June 22, 2022. https://www.researchgate.net/publication/23679811_What_We_Regret_Most_Are_Lost_Opportunities_A_Theory_of_Regret_Intensity

his life. Despite earning good marks in school, most of his teachers believed he was lazy —a daydreamer who posed questions that others couldn't fathom.

- Founding Father Benjamin Franklin left school at age 10 because his parents needed him to work to support the family. Yet he never stopped reading books as quickly as he found them, and is still regarded as one of the United States' most successful self-educated individuals.
- Another person who left school at a young age to support his family is Jim Carrey. He dropped out at age 15, and because his father, a musician who was usually employed, couldn't provide for the family, they lived in a van for a time. Still, Jim tenaciously held onto his dream of becoming a famous comedian one day and began doing stand-up comedy as a teenager in addition to holding down a number of jobs.
- Stephen King's wife encouraged him not to give up when *Carrie*, his first novel, was rejected more than 30 times. He finished it and has not stopped writing since; as they say, the rest is history.
- Oprah Winfrey ran away from her dysfunctional home at age 14 after being raped numerous times by family members and friends. Sadly, her young son died, but the young girl found the courage and temerity to go on to achieve high marks in high school and eventually won a contest with a speech she presented. For that, she was awarded a full college scholarship. No wonder she is such a strong proponent for young women and education.
- You've quite likely heard that Thomas Edison failed more than 1,000 times before inventing the first successful light bulb. He was fond of saying that he did

not consider those attempts to be failures, but rather that "The light bulb was an invention with 1,000 steps."
- Richard Branson received poor marks throughout his early schooling. Standardized tests were the bane of his educational career. Still, he persisted and by virtue of his personality and determination, went on to found the empire that is Virgin Air, Virgin Records, and several other multi-billion dollar companies.[7]

My kids don't know poverty as I do. They only know opportunity is everywhere.

There are countless more doctors, attorneys, sports figures, entertainers, writers, and people from all walks of life who stand as shining examples of where belief in oneself and a strong sense of purpose can lead. I encourage you not to be quick to judge someone's success, for you may have no idea how or where they started.

To move beyond a $1 million deficit and break the generational cycle of poverty, I sought advice from those around me. It piqued my curiosity, so I joined a UW community where I was included in its circle. Look out for successful circles. Learn to join in the circle. Show up. Participate. Contribute. Become part of the circle.

Leadership Lesson for Summer

Rope, Line & String Technique

Summer's energy fuels action, but like a kite in a strong breeze,

7. Jacques, Renee. "16 Wildly Successful People Who Overcame Huge Obstacles To Get There." Huffington Post. Accessed June 22, 2022. https://www.huffpost.com/entry/successful-people-obstacles_n_3964459

too much force can cause a crash. Our next lesson shows the power of finesse over force. I have spent every summer at the lake on the shores of Lake Winnipeg with my boys since they were born.

A big part of the summer revolves around ropes and lines and strings: boats, sailing, windsurfing, fishing rods and reels, stunt kites, and kiteboards.

My children have learned how to make and use various ropes, lines, and strings. I started discussing this subject with them immediately, even before they were out of diapers. Because this is one of life's greatest lessons, if you don't learn or fully understand it, you will miss every opportunity that comes your way.

What I mean is, pull too hard and you have a knot that you don't want and can't easily get out of. Or you pull the kite right out of the sky. Push too hard at the wrong time, and you get nothing. Don't push on a string, line, or rope—ever. Go with the flow. Slow down, breathe deeply, and focus. With gentle skill, handle the rope and line the string. Pay attention to the wind. Watch the sky and whatever you do—don't push on a rope.

> One small touch on the string at the right time will lead to remarkable results.

The leadership lesson here is that a rope is great for lifting or pulling. However, it is totally useless for pushing anything. Note how a rope interacts in the whole system. When you really want to achieve something in a highly complex system with lots of changing external and internal forces, you need to know how all the elements interact and play off of one another, and inevitably understand how the rope, the string, and the line serve you in achieving your goal.

If handled with the right finesse at the right time with the right energy, shifting and assessing changes in forces, a gentle pull can make everything happen exactly as you need or wish. Toe the line incorrectly, and you lose the fish. In sailing, the tighter the rope, the greater the wind. Pull the hand beams up the boat, or crash the kite.

My boys know these lessons better than most grown-ups. Everyone should learn this leadership skill. It is imperative. Pay attention to the external forecast at play. Prepare your system for ropes and knots. Know that all is well.

Summer Takeaways

Grow... yourself, your business. Summer and heat are the optimal times to grow larger and encompass the world around you.

Rejuvenate–rethink your assumptions, your ideas. Breathe new life into family and work. Rest. Relax. Restore. Grow.

Reconnect–communities come together in the summer. Families and work families have the chance to form deeper bonds that will carry them through the seasons.

Takeaways on Women and Burnout

1. Women experience greater burnout at work because they often have additional stress from unpaid work at home, such as caring for children or elderly parents. This makes it more difficult for them to remain in demanding careers.
2. Companies are missing out on many talented women employees. To fix this, they should offer more flexible ways of working - like part-time jobs, sharing jobs

between people, or letting employees pick which projects they want to do. This helps women better balance work and home life.

The Top 3 Strategies for Immersive Proximity:

1. Seek out successful environments: Placing yourself in areas where successful people gather, such as universities, business events, or community meetings, is crucial. This approach increases your chances of making meaningful connections and encountering opportunities.
2. Be visible: Ensuring that you're in a position where others can see you and potentially offer help or opportunities is vital. As the text emphasizes, you can't be helped if you're not seen. This involves actively participating in events and placing yourself in situations that allow you to interact with others. Speak up. Speak often about how you can help.
3. Adopt a learning mindset: Approaching new situations and interactions as a "passionate learner" is key. This attitude not only helps you engage more effectively with others but also makes you more approachable and interesting to potential connections. It opens doors to new relationships and combats isolation by fostering genuine interactions based on curiosity and growth.

These strategies form a powerful foundation by actively placing yourself in enriching social environments, making yourself known, and approaching interactions with an open, growth-oriented mindset. They also help you build momentum.

Leadership Snack Pack

Water Off a Duck's Back

If you encounter a setback, just overcome it. Shake it off. Don't sit in it for too long. Learn and move on. Shake it off. Just like water off a duck's back. Just keep swimming.

Conclusion: Summer — The Season of Expansion and Energy

Summer is a season of vibrant growth, energy, and connection. Nature is alive with sound and color, yet the intense heat also invites rest, daydreaming, and a slower pace. It reflects the passion and adventurous spirit of young adulthood—fueling both hard work and joyful play. Summer encourages relaxation, socializing, and deepening bonds with family and community, while also offering renewed drive and creativity. When balanced, its intensity can invigorate both personal life and business efforts.

I wish you a summer moment when you can see the fireflies dancing along the lakehouse screens and the moonlight dancing along the gentle ripples of the soft, rocking waves. And all you can hear is a gentle sploosh of the waves lapping against the rocks and every now and then a footstep of the woodland creatures: a fox, a bear, a wolf, a deer. The shadows and sparkles on the lake are more beautiful than any painting or picture.

If you can quiet your mind enough and be present in this summer moment, your soul connects you to the magical moment of summer restoration. And for that JOY. You grow. And heal. And rejoice in a quiet stillness of serenity. Remember this moment when times are turbulent. This dancing light on the moonlit lake shines brightly on you in ways that resonate deep within you. Find your moment of summer restoration.

Summer arrives with brightness, boldness, and an unmistakable surge of momentum. It is the season of growth in full display—a time when ideas blossom, teams flourish, and leaders feel the heat of both opportunity and responsibility. Summer leadership is vibrant and outward-facing. It calls you to stretch, to explore, and to take confident steps into bigger spaces.

In Summer, the days are long and possibility feels abundant. This is the moment to build on your progress, strengthen your influence, and cultivate experiences that energize both you and those you lead. Summer invites you to embrace movement, connection, and joy. It reminds you that leadership isn't only about discipline and direction—it is also about vitality, celebration, and courage.

As you close this chapter, imagine your own Summer and the energy it brings. Let these reflections help you shape a season infused with bold action and meaningful enjoyment.

Reflect on these questions as you design your Summer:

Who is in your Summer circle?

Who brings energy, innovation, and encouragement into your leadership? Who helps you think bigger, move faster, or laugh more freely?

What activities will you do?

What adventures, collaborations, or initiatives will define your Summer? Which pursuits will fuel your enthusiasm and expand your impact?

Where will you do them?

Picture the places that inspire your momentum—outdoor spaces, creative environments, lively meeting spots, or new territories you're ready to explore.

What songs are playing?

What soundtrack sets the pace for your Summer? What music lifts your spirit, sparks creativity, or drives your determination?

Your Top 3 Tasks You Must Accomplish

Identify the three essential goals that will mark a powerful Summer for you. What must you launch, build, or elevate before this season closes?

As you step into Summer, remember: this is the leadership season of expansion and energy. Let it propel you toward bold choices, memorable moments, and meaningful growth.

FALL

To Autumn

"Season of mists and mellow fruitfulness,
Close bosom-friend of the maturing sun;
Conspiring with him how to load and bless
With fruit, the vines that round the thatch-eves run;
To bend with apples the moss cottage-trees,
And fill all fruit with ripeness to the core;
To swell the gourd and plump the hazel shells
With a sweet kernel, to set budding more,
And still more, later flowers for the bees,
Until they think warm days will never cease,
For summer has o'er-brimm'd their clammy cells."

— John Keats, 1819[1]

Chinese Medicine associates the seasons with various elements. Fall is linked with metal and with the lungs. Fall is the season

1. Keats, John. "To Autumn." Poetry Foundation. Accessed June 12, 2022. https://www.poetryfoundation.org/poems/44484/to-autumn

that rules organization, creating limits, and honoring boundaries. It is the time of year to shift away from Summer's outward expansive nature toward greater introspection.

Fall is the perfect time to complete any projects begun in Spring or Summer. Take a deep breath and celebrate the rewards of your hard work. Fall also is about starting new projects that are directed more internally. It's a time to employ your body and mind even while focusing inward.

Emotions are definitely affected by the change of seasons, and it's natural for us to experience some sadness during the onset of the Fall. Just like the leaves drop from the trees to decompose upon the face of the earth, Fall can bring up feelings of loss. This can translate into a reminder of the cycle of life, our own fragility as humans and thoughts about our own mortality. If any sadness that arises remains suppressed or is unattended, it can morph into depression.

It is a crucial time to be mindful of all of this and to support body, mind, and spirit through healthy lifestyle choices. Hang out with positive friends, coworkers, and family members, and consider severing ties with anyone who is consistently negative. If you can't let them go (as in family members) then make it a point to shield yourself with white light energy when interacting with them, and simply refuse to take part in any snarky, negative talk. Change the subject, and if necessary, walk away.

Since the energy of the lungs is about "letting go," once autumn arrives, be mindful of releasing anything you may be holding onto tenaciously in order to create room for new experiences that will stimulate growth and learning.

Fall is about abundance and giving thanks for what we have. It is an active season in which we harvest the fruits of our labour.

2

"Autumn shows us how beautiful it is to let things go."

— UNKNOWN

Introduction to Fall

Autumn is synonymous with ripening. Trees are heavy with fruit and vegetables that were once the size of a button… now full-grown and ready to eat. Months of work culminate as farmers busy themselves with the harvest.

The warm days gradually fade, and the fields are picked clean. The air becomes cool and crisp, with a briskness that can be both invigorating and piercing. Fall's colors are a glorious celebration before we enter the period of dormancy.

This is a time of hurried movement and activity. Our actions can even acquire a frenetic quality, comparable to squirrels and chipmunks hurriedly gathering nuts for the long winter ahead. Yet Fall also possesses a spirit of creativity and inspiration that can prompt exciting new ideas.

In the same way that we prune fruit from the Summer crops, Fall is the time of year to prune away the excesses of Summer.[3] Above all, Fall presents the natural law of dynamic balance, urging us to weigh our harvest, consolidate our energy, and plan intentionally before the final darkness. Fall is a time to begin consolidating your energy and focus on the harvest.

---

2. Emma Suttie, D.Ac, AP . "Autumn/Fall." Chinese Medicine Living. Accessed June 12, 2022. https://www.chinesemedicineliving.com/nutrition/seasons/fall/

3. Lotus Leaf Acupuncture Website. "Welcoming the Season of Autumn." lotusleafacupuncture.com. Accessed July 15, 2022. https://www.lotusleafacupuncture.com/welcoming-the-season-of-autumn/

Our respiratory systems are vulnerable in the Fall, as cooler air and falling leaves and other plant matter can contribute to poor air quality. So it's important to do all you can to strengthen your immune system. Ellagic acid blocks the cancer-causing actions of many airborne pollutants, which are abundant in raspberries, blackberries, and other fruits.

Eat foods that support good health, such as immune-boosting root vegetables like cabbage, squash, and sweet potatoes. Some spices that are good for this are onions, garlic, turmeric, ginger, fennel, chili peppers, and rosemary.

Fresh nuts are a great source of vitamin E and fatty acids, specifically walnuts, almonds, pecans, and hazelnuts. Selenium is an immune-stimulating, cancer-protective mineral that's found in foods like butter, lamb, nuts, brown rice, and liver. Reishi Mushrooms are a mood enhancer; they can help alleviate anxiety and depression, and promote better sleep. It's essential to get adequate rest in the Fall.

My Memories of Fall

Winning Everything Always

In grade 8, I saw too much of the bottom. I slept on the floor, no bed. And the mice, I will never forget the mice. Sometimes running across me when I slept. I still have PTSD about mice. And what a scary, sad, lonely place to be. When people bottom out, it is incredibly dreary. The most appropriate word to describe it is hopeless. Hopelessness. No way out. Nothing to look forward to. Nothing to do. Nowhere to go. Surviving keeps people busy. There is no time to get ahead. Unless. You do one thing every day towards winning. Thriving is very different from surviving. When you see the bottom up close, you know you don't want to stay there for too long. I had made a habit of running everywhere I went, mostly because I was scared of the people in our neighborhood, or because I was cold, or late, or had no bus fare. When I went to St. John's School in the North End, a rather rough school, I ran there every day.

One cold morning, a coach there noticed me running to school and asked me if I wanted to join the track club. One thing I could do was run, and all I needed was a pair of running shoes, which I didn't get right away. Changed my life. Forever. I ran track and won everything, even when I had no business winning. I loved winning. I won numerous ribbons and medals, and it felt great to win. I ran track up until I went to University. It was an amazing, excellent escape from my awful circumstances.

My dad started doing better, too; he began to dig us out of the financial hole we were in. By the time I was in grade 9, I was winning all the time, and my dad had made enough money to move us to a better part of town. More good things came. The discipline I learned from my track coaches forever changed my life.

Conditioning and winning, practicing and winning, digging deeper and winning. Even if I lost, I would study what went wrong and what I needed to do differently or better so I could win next time. These coaches helped me understand how to win; they helped me break it down. This is when I learned about consistency and perseverance. Small changes can make significant outcomes. At the beginning of grade 9, we moved to the Burgundy house in Fort Garry, which backed onto the cemetery, and frightened me. I still ran in this neighborhood, even though I was no longer as afraid. It was an amazing place to be, the momentum of many positive things to come. Positives sprinkled in with lots of hard times.

I vividly remember curling weekly with my two sisters and my father in the mixed league, and my father often did not show up.

Curling, to me at the time, was not a sport at all; it was more like a social activity, like bowling. Why? Well, for one, everyone smoked on the ice, not me or my sisters, but most of the grown-ups and teenagers smoked on the ice; it was encouraged. There were even ashtrays at either end of the curling rink and even midway on each sheet of ice so you could smoke and sweep at the same time. The curlers also drank alcohol everywhere, on the ice and behind the glass.

I would have been around ten or eleven when I vividly remember the Turkey shoot. I made it to the finals, and everyone was watching, pressed up against the glass. I was competing against all ages, even grown-ups. The guy I was competing against smoked Player's Plain. I remember a giant ash fell off his smoke right onto the ice, and it melted a tiny hole.

Well, it caught my attention enough to distract me, but not enough to cause me to miss the button. I drew the last rock directly onto the button, and I won the turkey. Everyone seemed amazed. I just wanted the damn turkey and didn't want this smoking old guy to win the turkey. I was laser-focused and had been observing the ice closely all day. I was always very good at trend spotting. Anyway, it was really cool to be noticed for being good at something, even if it was curling. This was my first real taste of winning. I said to myself, "Winning is winning." Way better than losing. After that, I always wanted to win at everything.

Baby Blue AMC Concord Wagon, 5-door

At university, I drove a used baby-blue AMC Concord wagon. Well, this car was not easy to get for someone like me; mostly broke, trying to be an engineer, attending the most elite engineering school in Canada. I had no business attending UW, except that I am absolutely sure I was being carried by Angels during my time there. I was admitted to UW through my grit and the grace of the Dean of Engineering at the time, and the support of very kind administrative staff. You would think getting in was tough.

Well, attending, passing, and surviving the four and three-quarters years in a world so foreign to me it made my head spin. I managed to obtain student loans every year, although they were often delayed, and the amount was never sufficient for the term. I never had the luxury of living in residence, although I often thought about how fortunate those students were. Their parents even came every term to help move them in and out.

No one from my family ever came to Waterloo when I studied, no one even came to my graduation. Not a card, not a gift, no flowers from my family. Not surprised. My dad didn't believe me, and my mom and most of my family could not even imagine what I was doing.

My moving days each term were quite simple. No bed to move, no dresser, nothing heavy or bulky: a backpack, a few boxes, and my bike. At some point, I acquired a TV and a VCR. Although I also had some heavy blankets and pillows. I was quite used to sleeping on the floor.

Sometimes I could find a place to rent with a bed and afford to rent it for the term, but most often I could not. I relied heavily on the generosity of my new university friends, although I was always careful not to take too much or stay too long. I had to travel back and forth to Manitoba every four months to work, and the cost of the bus or a flight always stressed me out, mainly because, if I did the math, I could never afford it. Every term, I sold my books for the money and to travel light.

I had difficulty letting that Baby Blue AMC Concord Wagon go. I cried when the wrecker removed it. They paid me 50 dollars for the car. I took the 50 dollars and bought as much beer as I could and I drank it all, and pissed it all away. That car owed me nothing. That car saved my life. I always believed in the car and never worried. Looking back, knowing what I know about cars, angels is all I can say. I was being carried by angels.

Business Tips as Fall Approaches

In business, activating innovation and creating new methodologies, products, and services might be compared to various aspects of the four seasons, such as planting, tending, harvesting, and preparing the fields for the next planting time.[4]

In the Fall, it's critical that planning is completed and executed to sustain organizations through what can be a lean, tough Winter. Decision-makers must recharge and conserve their energy while strategizing what will be needed during the next months and for the next fiscal year. Creating sustainable resources and inventory is mandatory. Therefore, Fall is an optimal season during which change and innovation become crucial.[5]

Hearth and Home

As temperatures drop, we seek warmth. We pull out our favorite sweaters and gravitate towards hot soups and stews. Supportive, loving relationships help keep us grounded amidst the swirl of activity. Autumn holidays, celebrations, and school gatherings provide opportunities for families and communities to come together.

---

4. Cause It Website. "Business Model Innovation Season By Season." Causeit.org. Accessed July 10, 2022. https://www.causeit.org/business-model-innovation-through-the-seasons
5. Ibid.

Honoring the harvest is an important ritual with ancient roots. It has an archetypal quality that pertains not only to food but also to reaping the rewards of the year's efforts and recognizing the teamwork that made it possible. The enthusiasm of spring and the drive of summer culminate in the fall. Now we have the opportunity to step back and assess the fruits of our labor with pride and satisfaction. Fall is the ideal time to review and ensure we appreciate the work we have done.

While this season is synonymous with harvest, ripening, and abundance,[6]

it simultaneously represents the onset of decay and decline. Witnessed by falling leaves and tree limbs laid bare, fall can be associated with things said to be past their prime. The autumn of one's life, old age, and yes, even death itself. Summer, or prime, becomes associated with the past as one enters what is often referred to as the twilight of one's life.

As you journey through the seasons, there is no better time than Fall to reminisce about how you, your family, community, and workplace have fared.

> "Notice that autumn is more the season of the soul than of nature."
>
> — FRIEDRICH NIETZSCHE

---

6. Interesting Literature Website. "The Curious Symbolism of Autumn in Literature and Myth." Interestingliterature.com. Accessed July 10, 2022. https://interestingliterature.com/2021/11/autumn-symbolism-literature-mythology/

Natural Laws for Fall

Harvest

Fall is when nature harvests the results of her work. Seeds grow to fruit, the sun-warmed earth gives back plentifully; not to forget the animal feast. In all areas of life, it's a fact that if you don't tend to your harvest, it will go to waste. Harvesting is a work in its own right and should not be neglected in our relationships, our work, and our communities.

Were you aware that fall is the only season that has two names?[7] Three, actually. Fall and autumn we all know, but there was also a third name used in the 12th and 13th centuries in Middle English: "haerfest." This referred to the gathering of crops, and of course, eventually became "harvest" since the full moon that occurs closest to the autumn equinox is known as the harvest moon.

Even North America's economy is based on the Harvest. Summer break for schoolchildren historically stems from having children at home to help with the harvest.

People have forgotten this was built for a reason, and it is set up the way it is to support the natural needs around the farm family.

Of course, this practice has evolved over many years. However, we must remember that the community, social, and economic structures were built around the natural cycle and the growing seasons.

---

7. Booth, Jessica. "25 Things You Never Knew About Fall." Redbook. October 6, 2020. https://www.redbookmag.com/life/g28999486/things-you-never-knew-about-fall/?slide=1

Celebration

Bear in mind that Fall is not just about reaping the rewards of hard work. Our rhythm-sensitive brains also need celebrations to mark the passing of time. It's important to be grateful for whatever we have grown with our own hands, take nothing for granted. Celebrations also bring us closer, wherever they take place and for whatever reason.

Movement

This is the time to get ready for Winter. With temperatures dropping, no one can afford to stay still. You will need all your acumen to prepare and ensure you survive winter.

My Seasonal Lesson

It was during my son's Sunday school that I got one of the most powerful lessons as a young mother—the one that ushered me into my season of Fall and into action.

At the time, I was living in Waterloo, Canada, and every Sunday, I would take my kids to the St. Louis church on Allen Street. That was during a particularly difficult period of my life. My husband was cheating on me and left the kids and me. I was more alone than ever. I never knew if I would be able to pay the bills or even feed my kids at the end of the day.

The beautiful cathedral and its wonderful choir had become a place of solace—a refuge. It was where I would vent my agonies at the end of each week. I remember the strange gazes of the congregation as I stood there, crying, squeezing my young sons' tiny hands. I was confused by the looks of irritation that my tears garnered.

After the service, I would take Robbie, a wonderful toddler and Cash, my dear baby to Sunday school. That one hour was my time to reflect, to breathe, to pause from the busyness of keeping my kids safe and happy. I would sit in the pews, praying to God for strength.

I would sit there every Sunday, crying and praying, until a strange incident happened that rattled my very soul.

One day, I lingered too long in the pew. I guess I was feeling too tired and tear-stained to get up, the heaviness of life pressing me down. I should have gone to get the boys, but instead, I just sat in the pew crying and crying. After what seemed like a long time, a withered elderly man came up to me. He could barely stand up. His hands trembled and he looked mad as hell. This was more than I could handle at the moment. All I could think was, "*Good God. Get this guy away from me.*"

The old man grabbed my arm with his cold, frail fingers and yelled, "What is wrong with you? What are you so sad about? What on earth could you possibly be crying for?"

And in between sobs, I told that old, terrifying man all my truth: "I am alone. My husband left me. My family is not here, and they do nothing to help me. I'm broke. I can't feed my kids or pay my bills, and I don't know what is going to happen next, and I am scared and sad all at the same time."

The man stood there, incomprehensible anger filling his gaze. And then he reprimanded me. "Oh. You're scared and sad, are you? Is that so? My wife is dead. My friends are dead. My body is broken. My only son died at birth. I have nothing to look forward to, and I have no more life left in me. Every Sunday, I look at you with your two beautiful boys. I watch you cry, and I say to myself, 'This girl must be crazy…'

You piss me off. I remember when I was young and had decades ahead of me. How exciting that you don't know what will happen, and you don't know what to do. You have your whole life ahead of you. You are young and beautiful, and your boys are beautiful."

That man literally told me to smarten up.

He went on, "And for God's sake, pick something, and it will be better than what you are doing. See your sons and make every day a better day for them. Somehow, by God's grace, you have life to look forward to." With those words, he let go of my arm, smiled at me, and walked away.

I never saw him at church again, but his words still rang through my mind and soul. His words helped me change my perspective and attitude toward life slightly each day.

I still cry in church, though, as soon as the choir starts—old habits and all that. I don't mind as long as I never forget to be grateful for my life and my accomplishments.

So why do I share this story? Because this experience was like the first cool breeze of the coming fall, it awoke me and prompted me to reflect on my own personal 'harvest'. His words opened the doors, and gratitude and joy rushed in. I was ready to act.

The Five-Ingredient Recipe for Leadership Success

When you are all prepared and ready to act in the Fall season, how should you go about it in the most effective way?

1. Political support. It could be small or big, but it's the community and political support. You must assess the

political dimension of what you are trying to achieve. Even in my own family, if I'm going to go do something, I've got to make sure I've got the family support, community support, and support at work. Whatever the circle. Support is better than no support.

2. Get the science right. What I mean by that is the facts, figures, business model, and revenue model. The numbers don't lie. You must have a business model in operation or one that's going to fly. You must have a clear and decisive plan for your goals. Whether that involves ensuring you reach growth and sales targets, adapting your business to different revenue streams, marketing strategies, or products, or consolidating your family's winter plans. If the numbers indicate you must reduce your business expenses, do so in every way possible. Although Spring is the best time to make workforce reductions or terminate those who are not aligned or are not contributing productively, Fall is another opportunity to reevaluate this issue. Fall is a time for harvest, abundance, and gratitude to come together. Have gratitude for yourself. Count your blessings.
3. Nail the communications and education side. You need to manage up, manage side-to-side, and manage below. Everyone has to come along for the ride and the journey, which has an educational component and a communication component. Build a construct. Bring everybody along for the ride.
4. Monitor what you have. Collect data and determine if what you are doing is working or not working; decide whether you're on the right track or not. When you monitor and collect data, you evaluate, and then you adapt, adjust and integrate. You don't just set it and forget it. Like a family, you have to hold it, carry it, and

watch it. Like a baby's feeding schedule, it changes. You just nailed it, and now the feeding has changed. No problem. Now, you have to monitor, adjust, integrate, and listen.

5. Build a cross-section of the community. Appoint a representative for each subject; someone who represents each subject matter that's coming together. The success of the relationship is the primary goal, but each individual also has their own smaller goal.

Here are some suggestions to boost Fall spirit in your workplace:

- As the season approaches and the weather begins to cool, several nonprofit organizations, including shelters, will need additional assistance and resources to help individuals cope with the elements. Choose an organization to support, and create a team that will take time to serve in ways that best assist the recipient group. Some ideas to consider include food and clothing drives, volunteering at shelters, reading to children, and those who are vision-impaired. By bringing the teams together, many other valuable contributions can be made.
- Create a company Oktoberfest, complete with Bavarian food and drink, outdoor team games, and German music.
- Hold a craft fair where employees can buy and sell their creations. Promote this to the community and offer prizes to encourage public participation.
- Hold meetings outdoors, weather permitting. The fresh, crisp Fall air can be extremely exhilarating and inspiring!

In my office, I line up with the quarters – Q1, Q2, Q3, Q4. We put our heads down, we work like crazy, and then we celebrate. We celebrate small things, but it's the rhythm, the cadence of the season. Businesses follow that cadence, but they miss giving enough space to marinate, stew, percolate and celebrate.

> Expect to have hope rekindled. Expect your prayers to be answered in wondrous ways. The dry seasons in life do not last. The spring rains will come again.
>
> — SARAH BAN BREATHNACH

Seasonal cadence is a common practice in business marketing, grounded in the ubiquitous strategy of planned obsolescence. You've got to give that creative process to the business rhythm. Many founders, CEOs, and Boards are constantly just drilling for more and more. To get the best out of your team, you've got to make seasonal sprints. You make a sprint in the rhythm of the season, then you reflect, take it in and celebrate, and then go again as per the season. That's the seasonal pace most businesses are missing, that natural cadence that should be there.

The companies that do it inadvertently get the best out of people–higher performance and better outcomes.

Find balance, align the seasonal rhythm, and make a plan.

When Fall comes around the corner, I think, "I have to make a plan for the next 12 months." Really focus on each season. Align with the seasonal rhythm and the expectations of the season. Be sure to take notice: is this a rest-and-restore season? Or is this a take action season?

This ritual first appeared when I was searching for my logo more than 25 years ago. I ended up with something that reflects the balance between light and dark, yin and yang. That is what the Fall equinox is about—the balance of the shifting, tipping season, the finely balanced point beyond which we tumble into ever more darkness.

All the way to the following equinox in the Spring. And round and round again, from one seesaw to the next. In my mind, this dynamic balance is the ideal moment to set the program for the next 12 months. When September comes, I plan to set this balance and build on it in the coming months. Being intentional and aware of each season's pace, tradition, and natural rhythms.

> Fall, no matter if your business is in Q1 or Q2, signifies a natural starting point.

People move out of their vacation mood and mode, and kids start school. Everybody is coming off summer, vacations, and a natural grind begins. They're walking into the office, and there's a new amount of friction. There's this tension where people are thinking, "We have so much to do!"

Even if your Q1 is in January, September still finds you in a state of flurried activity; this tension of everything being off-balance and off-kilter. This fall period is a time to find your balance. It's time to say, "What is our plan from now until the end of June? Because that's when we're going on our summer break again."

Answer these questions: Why? What? When? Where? Who?

It's the idea that the best-laid plans must be balanced, realistic, and have the right amount of tension. But if it's off-kilter, everybody just blows up, and we get nothing done. Always base this on the five W's.

My job as a leader was always to create an executable plan with a balanced approach. I would go to my board and say, "This is balanced. I've balanced this with all of the competing interests. I'm balancing all of the stakeholders."

Action

Oddly enough, Fall is also the running season. It's the salmon run. If you just look at nature, there's a lot of hurried readiness, because many animals are about to go into hibernation. We will soon enter a period of dormancy. It's also harvest time. We have to get the wheat, corn, and everything off the fields before it freezes. It's a stressful race against the axis's clock of the turning planet.

You can get your people to run like crazy if you know the five W's., but only if you've achieved balance. If you find yourself, as a leader, pushing too hard at the wrong time, you'll get a revolt. But when you see that perfect rhythm of what people can achieve, they know they can achieve it, you've assembled the right team—that's when you know you've put enough resources into it. People settle in, and then they just… run. Achievements and clarifications to follow.

Communicating Up

Organizations suffer when key people can't effectively influence up. Most people are focused on effort rather than results. They worry over what the organization or their boss owes them, should do for them, and they obsess over the authority they '*should have*,' thus rendering themselves ineffective.

Although knowledge workers may know more about their work than their managers do and have years of education and experience, they may not know how to influence upward effectively.

When communication in business doesn't flow effectively both ways, many aspects of the organization suffer. Therefore, holding regular meetings where all levels of the business can share insights and experiences can avoid such pitfalls as:

- An uptick in employee turnover.[8] Retaining employees may seem costly and time-consuming, but research indicates that replacing an employee can cost up to three times their salary. When companies embrace and practice effective communication, they are 50% more likely to experience turnover levels below the industry average.
- A drop in customer service levels. When employees are not provided with adequate information to perform quality service, the customers suffer as well as the company's reputation. Additionally, customers sense low employee morale, which amplifies the problem.
- Plummeting employee productivity. Do they know the five W's?
- Higher risk of injury when health and safety hazards are not communicated effectively.
- A rise in absenteeism.[9] Even if employees are not quitting their jobs, poor communication may strongly influence them to call in sick more often. When employees feel adequately informed, absenteeism tends to decline.

It's patently obvious that failing to communicate both up and down effectively impacts the bottom line of any business.

---

8. Wells, Kristen. "6 Effects of Poor Communication in Business." FSD. November 8, 2017. https://fsd.servicemax.com/2017/11/08/6-business-impacts-poor-communication/
9. Ibid.

Communication skills are paramount to productivity and the overall health of organizations.

Even the greatest wisdom and knowledge not applied to action render themselves meaningless.

What can you do?

1. When presenting ideas, realize that it is your responsibility to sell, not theirs to buy. Great salespeople take responsibility for achieving results, refusing to blame their customers for not buying their products.
2. By developing your ability to present ideas and not blaming management for not adopting them, you accomplish much more. An effective upward influencer must be a good teacher.
3. Use a business case approach to present the ROI.

Good teachers realize that communicating knowledge is often a greater challenge than possessing knowledge.

Bottomline: don't shy away from your responsibilities, own your actions and you will not only become a healthier, more effective person yourself, you will also positively influence your organization and those working around you.

Community

Fall is unique among all the seasons because of the many celebrations it encloses in its cool arms. It's a season ripe with opportunities to come closer. through food, through the expression of gratitude; through the sheer cold in the air that pushes us indoors, but at the same time reminds us that winter is coming, and without our community to support us, we might not make it.

Celebrating the harvest

Celebrations were always and still are what bring a community together. It's what ties loose strands of people into a closely woven whole. The fall celebration is generally the harvest. That's true for communities, as well as for business. For example, if Apple announces its product launch in September, it is harvesting. They're hitting an extra Christmas.

Harvest time is ingrained into my being because of my rural farming roots. But I carried that with me into my business world, and I knocked it out of the park over and over again. Recognition and rewards, gratitude and appreciation. Seeds along the way, in creating and maintaining a positive culture.

Fall Rituals

Either at home or at work, we need to belong somewhere, and there's no better way to feel like you belong than to share rituals with the people closest to you. You don't have to search for a community. By establishing rituals in every aspect of your life, you are creating a community around you.

You have to build your community. It all starts with microcosms of little communities. We've had small projects, like a centennial celebration. The team we assembled built a small community around it. When people are part of something that feels like a community, they work so hard for you. They are so passionate. Each contributor matters. The community is strongest when every part is recognized. The sum of the parts is what matters.

If you give them responsibility but also give them some authority —autonomy—to run and some space, that's the magical part. It can be done on a small scale or a big scale. It works. It just works. In a sense, you create the place, and then people rush to fill it in. Identify a common goal and collaborate to achieve it.

Ancient Cultures: Fall Rituals and Ceremonies

For millennia, people have celebrated the Fall equinox. In the Northern Hemisphere, the September equinox coincides with harvest, and many ancient harvest celebrations occur on or around the Fall equinox.[10]

Here are just a few of the many cultures that celebrate this time of year:

In ancient Greece, the September equinox marked the return of the goddess Persephone to the underworld, where she is reunited with her husband, Hades, for several months.

The ancient Chinese began celebrating the Harvest Moon Festival centuries ago, during the Shang Dynasty. Part of their celebration involved making offerings to the moon for a good harvest of wheat and rice.

Higan is celebrated by some Japanese Buddhists, and occurs twice a year - once during the Fall equinox, and again during the Spring. The translation of "Higan" is "from the other shore of the Sanzu," which, in Buddhist tradition, refers to the passage into the afterlife by crossing the mythical Sanzu. For Higan, Japanese Buddhists often return to their hometowns to honor their ancestors.

Many people in the United Kingdom have celebrated Fall Harvest festivals since the times of the druids and pagans. It is typically held on the Sunday that falls closest to the Harvest

---

10. History.com Website. "Fall Equinox." History.com. August 15, 2019. https://www.history.com/topics/natural-disasters-and-environment/fall-equinox

Moon. Pilgrims carried this tradition with them to America, and it is thought to have contributed to what became Thanksgiving.

During the French Revolution, the French government designed and adopted a new annual calendar. The New Year would start at midnight on the date of the autumnal equinox. The revolutionaries sought to eliminate religious or royalist influences and named each month after a natural element. This was followed from 1793 until Napoleon abolished it in 1806.

Modern Vietnamese and Ethnic Chinese people still celebrate the Harvest Moon. During the mid-Autumn Festival, family and friends gather to give thanks, share food and observe the moon. Round pastries called mooncakes are traditionally enjoyed during this time.[11]

Action: Introduce season-appropriate rituals at your business. Food is a great place to start.

Case study– "The problem – The vision – The team"

This is a lesson on how staying grounded and focusing on what really matters can breed miracles.

I was in charge of all the engineers across the entire province of Ontario. Frank Ingratta was there at the time I was there. He was the Deputy Minister in charge of the Ministry of Agriculture, Food, and Rural Affairs. He hired me when there were 5000 employees. He knew everybody's name.

After he hired me, the first thing he did was schedule a luncheon with me. His secretary opened his door, I entered his palatial corner C-Suite office, and we broke bread together. He had a

11. Ibid.,

wonderful meal planned, and the entire dinner centered on the ritual of breaking bread.

I started there in the Fall, so he showed me the bounty of all of these local farmers. The entire meeting consisted of his asking me questions. It was not he who was preaching to me about the business. He asked, "What do you think the single biggest issue is facing rural Ontario right now?" I said, "The economy. The brand. I think the rural countryside is going through an incredible challenge of going from family farms to corporate farms, and there's a lot of tension there. I think they're having an identity crisis."

We were having soup, and he asked, "What would you do about it?" I said, "Well, I'd create a new economy." He replied, "That will be your first assignment. Go do that."

We created the Green Energy Strategy for the Province of Ontario in 18 months. We fundamentally changed the rural economy. If you drive across the Province of Ontario now, you'll see windmills, anaerobic digesters, and solar. We identified the problem and then developed the vision. I built a roundtable community quilt across multiple ministries and subject-matter experts.

We launched it in the Spring. I got a Bravo Award for creating innovation and vision for the Province of Ontario. We created this cross-section of various government layers and laid out the blueprint for how to change the rural countryside. It fundamentally changed the landscape of Ontario, and every subsequent province followed elements of that blueprint.

The problem – The vision – The team. The team, under my facilitation, developed an executable plan. We then implemented, measured, monitored, adjusted, and continued to fine-tune it. It continues to operate today as a continually improved program, with contributions from stakeholders.

I just put that on repeat for Market Square in Swift Current when the heart of the downtown was stale and depleted. What's the problem? The heart of the city is sick. Let's fix the heart. We'll build a market. We'll give them a reason to gather.

Downtown Swift Current had a very high vacancy. So many buildings were boarded up. I returned to the first principles of the notion of church: church, as a gathering of people. I said to myself, "We have to give people a reason to gather. How do you heal?" It's a recipe for repetition, but it is intended to build community. When there's a problem, put experts on it. Put the right experts on it. Give them a reason to gather.

That's what the harvest is. It's a gathering.

University

This is a story of how I learned never to let an opportunity pass me by; how I reached out and leaned in to secure my fall start at U of W.

Some people start at 0. Other people, the *lucky ones*, start at plus one million. I started at minus one million. What do I mean by that? My mom left abruptly when I was 8 years old. My father was mostly absent, either at work or out gambling, leaving us six children to fend for ourselves, always. We were three girls and three boys. I was the second-oldest, and as I said, when Mom left, my youngest brother was still in diapers.

I'm far from the "Lone Ranger" in my early experiences, and I realized this as I entered young adulthood. You may well have had a tough beginning yourself, yet you kept going and rose above those circumstances.

I was late for school every single day. I never told anyone why. I was ashamed, but I didn't want to share. The risk was always that Child and Family Services would conduct an investigation. Our lives played out under the constant fear that we would be sent to foster care. I earned straight As, even though I often had to stay home to care for my other siblings.

But I found a way to persevere: I would make deals with my teachers. I didn't have anything to barter, so I would negotiate washing the desks in the entire school to make up for being late or absent. This way I was able to graduate and obtain my diploma.

I learned at a young age to take care of myself as best I could. My mom had left us, predominantly because she was crazy. In a way, I understand what could have driven her crazy. A bad economy, no support. Some might argue that she didn't care enough, although that is highly unlikely. And debatable. What makes someone go crazy? Hopelessness. End of story. No hope. No help. No hero.

It can take enormous strength, dedication, and patience to work for a better life, and even then, it may not be enough to attain a more promising situation.

Especially when you're coming from generations and generations that add up to your minus million.

But I didn't come empty-handed to this struggle with life. Yes, my parents couldn't be depended on. Yes, our life was harsh. However, gaining insight into this and awareness of my circumstances proved to be a significant advantage for me.

Knowing how harsh life can be has given me perspective. Living in Rural Manitoba taught me Mother Nature's secrets. She provided me with the stability I lacked. And ever since then, the seasons remind me of that truth. That no matter where we are in life, the snow will fall again and the sunflowers will bloom.

You'll get a glimpse of the power those life lessons and nature taught me if you think of where I was then and where I am now. I am deeply grateful to them and for being where I am today.

I was not supposed to amount to anything. In Grade 3, I was told I was retarded. I could not read or write. If I were really lucky and worked really hard, I might make it as a waitress. That was what I was told. University, for sure, was a no-go. I grew up hearing just that.

I didn't want to be forever entrenched in this wicked, hard life. A farmer told me once, "You work hard at it, and it is easy; you work easily at it, and guess what? It is hard." That really stuck with me. All I needed was a slight nudge.

And I got it, in Grade 8, after everyone had given up on me, I had a wonderful teacher who told me that he believed in me. He just said it once as he looked at me with kind, supportive eyes. That was probably the first time I felt appreciated rather than judged, even though I was a mess. He didn't have to say it a second time.

Grade 8 was also the year I ran. Everywhere. Some coaches noticed me, so I joined the track team, and I won every event.

By the time I hit Mr Tulloch's physics class in Grade 10, I could close my eyes and read. I could do math equations in my head without having been taught how. I got 100% in physics. I honestly willed myself to learn. I didn't want to be considered retarded. I didn't want to be humiliated anymore.

I was admitted to a university. I went to McGill for physics. It was a win, but it was awful. I was broke the whole time, and I never felt so alone as when I was in a crowd in Montréal.

And so, back to Manitoba. I had broken out, but barely. The pull of the place and my generational history seemed too strong. I was beaten down, lost, and ready to give up. So, I went back to the place where I had felt good about myself, Mr. Tulloch's physics class. Crying, I asked Mr. Tulloch, "What the hell am I to do? I am broke and scared of big cities."

I knew I needed a small campus with a community, ideally a farming community, so I could relate. I also needed to earn money and attend school, but not simultaneously. He had the Waterloo University "Gear Up" poster on his wall, featuring a bicycle and its gears. He informed me that the University of Waterloo has a co-op program. Civil Engineering. This would be perfect for me.

I completed an application and submitted it. Nothing. Absolutely nothing.

So I called and called and called. Nothing.

If I could meet the decision-maker and ask them in person, they would have to give me a chance.

I practiced a speech. I went to the thrift store and bought the most studious skirt I could find, along with a navy blazer with brass buttons, flat black patent shoes, a cream colored blouse, a backpack, a notebook, and a pen

You work hard at it, and it is easy; you work easily at it, and it is hard, right?

After a long time, I managed to book a short meeting with the Dean. I didn't mention to the secretary that I was currently in Winnipeg, Manitoba, a 24-hour Greyhound bus ride away.

I arrived at the UW gates the next day. I informed the guard that I was meeting with the Dean of Engineering in hopes of gaining admission for September.

I found the Carl Pollock Building and the Dean's office. There was a bustle of busy engineering students. The energy of the place was nothing I had ever seen before, yet it was still very intimate.

I took a deep breath, walked in, and informed the staff member that I was there to see the Dean of Engineering. She looked puzzled. Then she said, "Oh, I am so sorry, he has gone home for the day. You will have to come back tomorrow."

I said okay. I felt hot. I didn't have hotel money. I only had my bus ticket back to Winnipeg and ten dollars. That's it. My dreams were dashed.

I turned on my heel and walked out. And then I stopped myself and gave myself shit. "You have already failed. What the hell. Just tell her. Beg."

So I turned back and told her the truth. She immediately called the Dean at home. "How quickly can you get back?" she asked.

I waited an hour for the Dean to return. The longest hour of my life. Waiting, trying to look normal, as I belonged.

When the Dean came, I recited my speech. He listened. I had practiced it so many times, I thought it was perfect. But then I noticed him rustling papers. And opening cabinet drawers like he was not even listening. I hoped he at least had questions, I had so much more to add, but my stomach was heavy with the feeling of failure.

The Dean indeed had one question: "Which program and when do you want to start?"

I sat there dumbfounded. He went on, "Civil or Mechanical, Electrical or Geological? Which program and when do you want to start?"

I'll tell you this. I learned this much in life: when someone says yes, shut your damn mouth and say thank you.

Civil. September. Thank you.

He filled out the paperwork on the spot and signed it. "Bring this with you in September. Welcome to UW."

I did three cartwheels in the hallway and called my mom.

And, wow, did I ever sleep on the long bus ride home!

From that day forward, I was finally at zero instead of minus a million. I had broken the generational chains that threatened to hold me back. I worked hard all Summer, and come September, I was ready for fall.

That one conversation changed my life. How many such discussions have you had in your life? Were you hard-pressed enough to pay attention when they happened?

Leadership Lesson – All the Right People at the Right Time

Do not schedule a meeting if the decision-maker cannot attend.

The right people need to be present. Do an assessment of who are key decision-makers, and who are key influencers. Be sure they are able to make it. Otherwise, inertia will allow a non-key man to sway the masses, and leadership will be abdicated to them rather than to the decision-makers.

"Whichever way the wind blows" is not a wise move. I have seen far too many decisions made by the wrong people at the wrong time. In an effort to hurry up… slow down. Make sure all the key people can attend the meeting the first time, especially if it is a huge important meeting, like setting the scope. If you want to see everything go to hell, go ahead with the meeting without the right people. Yikes.

Ask yourself, "Are all the key people able to come? Why are they important to the process? Are you okay moving without them? How important is their voice in the process?" If it is imperative, rebook or reschedule and trust the process.

If the doctor cannot perform the surgery, can you proceed without the doctor to save time? Absolutely not! Reschedule for a time when the physician is available. Don't let the janitor do your surgery.

> "Fall has always been my favorite season. The time when everything bursts with its last beauty as if nature had been saving up all year for the grand finale."
>
> — LAUREN DESTEFANO

Fall Takeaways

Problem-solving and vision creation can lead to major changes. The example of developing Ontario's Green Energy Strategy demonstrates how identifying a problem, creating a vision, and assembling the right team can transform an entire region's economy and landscape.

Revitalizing communities often requires giving people a reason to gather. The Swift Current market square project demonstrates how creating a central gathering place can breathe new life into a dying downtown area.

Fall is a time for both celebration and preparation. Many cultures have harvest festivals during this season, but it's also important to prepare for the coming winter - both physically and mentally.

Self-care practices for body, mind, and spirit become especially crucial as the days grow shorter and colder.

Celebrating Ancient Fall Ritual Takeaways

Many cultures worldwide have celebrated the Fall equinox for thousands of years. These celebrations often revolve around the harvest, giving thanks, and honoring ancestors.

Although these celebrations originate from different places and times, they share common themes. Many involve observing the moon, eating traditional foods, and spending time with family and friends.

Self-care Takeaways

Taking care of yourself during Fall is really important because it is a very busy time. This means looking after your body, mind, and feelings. Some good ways to do this are writing in a journal, exercising, and talking to a therapist if you need to.

What you eat and drink can affect how you feel. It is advisable to be careful with substances like coffee, sugar, and alcohol. Instead, drink lots of water, eat cooked foods (especially green vegetables), and try to get enough sleep. These things can help you feel better as the weather gets colder and the days get shorter.

Balancing the Energy of Autumn

Since Fall ushers in a certain level of melancholy, it's vital to attend to body/mind/spirit in every way possible. I've shared some suggestions about foods and supplements earlier in this section, so here I want to add a few more tips about taking care of your spiritual, mental, physical and emotional balance.

Self-Care Suggestions

- Schedule some therapy sessions to shift and balance your emotions.
- Start journaling. Use the page as a catharsis; offload your thoughts, memories, emotions. Tell your story. Put it on paper to free your mind and embrace new, positive ideas.
- Move your body! Dance, walk in the sunshine, do yoga, lift weights... Those memories and emotions are stored in your cells as sense memory. Engage with them to heal.

Mental self-care suggestions:

- Make to-do lists and cross 50% off before even getting started!
- Celebrate small progress towards a goal. Break big projects down into bite-sized chunks you can accomplish with more ease.
- Rest. Rest. Rest.
- Move your body. Vigorous exercise stimulates endorphin release and helps burn up excess neurotransmitters that are agitating and anxiety-provoking.

Body self-care suggestions:

- Approach caffeine, sugar, and alcohol with caution. Yes, all of those pumpkin spice drinks are delicious, but everything in moderation, remember? Caffeine and sugar are stimulating and may worsen your experience with anxiety and reduce your stress resilience. Alcohol robs your body of nutrients needed to bounce back when stressed.

- Stay hydrated. Water, broth, and herbal teas count. Caffeinated beverages and alcohol put you in a negative balance so you'll need to drink more to account for those.
- Ideally, exercise at about 50–70% of your capacity, breathing through your nose the entire time. And remember to balance your activity with adequate relaxation and sleep so that your tissues, cells, and muscles can rejuvenate properly.
- Practice good sleep hygiene and give yourself ample time to wind down at the end of the day so you're ready to sleep by the time your head hits the pillow.
- Epsom salt baths provide magnesium and sulfur to the muscles and joints, reducing muscle and joint pain. Add 2 cups to a warm bath and soak for 30+ minutes for maximum benefit.
- Eat cooked foods. These are easier to digest and will help ease any discomfort you might be feeling in your gut. Eat dark, leafy greens every day - preferably steamed rather than raw.

Finally, Fall is a season of preparation. Most Northerners experience some level of seasonal depression, which has been exacerbated since the onset of the pandemic and limited socializing. In addition to finishing house projects and getting things in order for a rejuvenating Winter, consider self-care techniques you can employ to nourish your mood through the cold, dark months ahead. Simple things like supplementing with vitamin D, cultivating a gratitude practice and drafting a list of nice things you can do for others can go a long way in lifting you up on every level.

Harvest–time to reap everything you've worked so hard for.

Celebrate – create your own rituals and share them with your community.

React–be mindful and active during this season. Prepare for the winter.

Leadership Snack Pack

- Daily Reflection: Spend 5 minutes each day reflecting on your leadership decisions and their impact.
- Inspirational Quote: "The greatest leader is not necessarily the one who does the greatest things. He is the one who gets the people to do the greatest things." – Ronald Reagan.
- Quick Read: Read a chapter from a leadership book or listen to a leadership podcast for fresh insights.
- Team Engagement Tip: Schedule a brief, informal check-in with your team to boost morale and maintain connection.
- Personal Development Task: Identify one skill you want to improve this month and create a plan to work on it regularly.
- Feedback Exercise: Ask for feedback from a colleague or mentor to gain new perspectives on your leadership style.

Conclusion Fall — The Season of Gathering and Grounding

As the colors deepen and the pace of the world subtly shifts, Fall invites you to pause with intention. It is a season that blends action with appreciation—a time to harvest what you've worked toward, gather the people who matter, and prepare thoughtfully for what comes next. Leadership in Fall is not loud or urgent; it is deliberate, relational, and reflective. It asks you to look at what you've built, honor your progress, and create rhythms that sustain you.

You are entering a season where the air itself seems to tell you: *Slow down enough to see clearly. Focus deeply enough to finish well.* This is the time to strengthen your circle, align your priorities, and commit to what truly matters. As you close this chapter, take a moment to imagine your own Fall—its atmosphere, its people, its textures, and its soundtrack. Let these reflections guide your leadership choices in the months ahead.

Remember these questions as you define your Fall:

Who is in your Fall circle?

Who brings steadiness, wisdom, or warmth to this season of your leadership? Who helps you think more clearly, work more effectively, or dream more courageously?

What activities will you do?

What rituals, routines, or projects will anchor your next steps? What practices help you gather your energy, harvest your progress, or prepare for future growth?

Where will you do them?

Picture your Fall settings—offices, living rooms, cafés, walking trails, quiet corners. Where will you do your best reflecting, connecting, and completing?

What songs are playing?

What music sets the tone for your Fall? What soundtrack helps you stay focused, grounded, or inspired as you lead?

Your Top 3 Tasks You *Must* Accomplish

List the three essential commitments or objectives that will define a successful Fall for you. What must be finished, refined, or secured before this season ends?

As you step forward, remember: Fall is the leadership season of clarity and completion. Let it shape not just what you do—but how intentionally and meaningfully you do it.

WINTER

IT SIFTS FROM LEADEN SIEVES

It sifts from leaden sieves,
It powders all the wood,
It is filled with alabaster wool
The wrinkles of the road.
It makes an even face
Of mountain and of plain —
Unbroken forehead from the east
Unto the east again.

It reaches to the fence,
It wraps it, rail by rail,
Till it is lost in fleeces;
It flings a crystal veil
On stump and stack and stem, —
The summer's empty room,
Acres of seams where harvests were,
Recordless, but for them.

It ruffles wrists of posts,
As ankles of a queen, —

Then stills its artisans like ghosts,
Denying they have been.

~ Emily Dickinson[1]

Taking it at surface value, yes, Winter is the coldest season. Winter embodies peace, reflection, introspection, rest and quiet. The natural rhythm of life slows, and it goes against our physiology to fight it. To quote Thoreau: 'Live in each season as it passes; breathe the air, drink the drink, taste the fruit, and resign yourself to the influences of each.'

The major holidays of the year occur during Winter, which makes sense because Winter is about aligning your inner values and core strength. The other three seasons tend to send you off on your separate ways, largely because your energy strives to move outward then. But family and community holiday meals and gatherings in Winter are a time of collaboration and celebration.

The snows come, blurring the edges of the world we know with a monotony of white. A sense of stillness pervades as winter cloaks the earth in a soft, luminous hush. It's almost like being at church.

Everything slows down. The natural world enters a state of suspended animation and instinctively adapts. If we listen closely, we can almost hear nature murmur, "Rest and renew. Rest and renew."

With the sun so far away, it is an opportune time to shine light into our lives. The cold months are punctuated with bursts of color and activity. Celebrations remind us that life is meant to be

1. Dickinson, Emily. "It Sifts from Leaden Sieves." Poets.org. Accessed June 12, 2022. https://poets.org/poem/it-sifts-leaden-sieves-31At face1

celebrated as we extend goodwill into our communities and the world beyond. There is something about this season that makes us more aware of our blessings.

Winter provides time and space to strengthen ties with loved ones. Talking, baking, watching movies, playing games, or sitting together by a fire have a way of restoring and rejuvenating relationships. The rhythm also provides an opportunity to reconnect with oneself. Surrendering to contemplation is both fitting and wise.

Whereas the surrounding months are bustling with activity and ongoing planning for activities and cottage getaways, Winter offers a quieter atmosphere and shorter days. These lend to more opportunities for rest and introspection. A simultaneous decrease in social events and an increase in routine activities means more time and dedication for self-work, along with the advancement and reconsolidation of your business and career.

Winter's measured tempo means plodding along steadily in your work. The introspective quality of the season offers an opportunity to gain perspective on our progress and visions for the future. Give your ideas time to incubate.

Introduction to Winter

There is more to Winter than bitter cold, stark landscapes, and numbing wetness. Just as trees lay their branches bare, this season is a time for us to focus on what truly matters. To bare our souls, to cut away anything that unnecessarily drains our power, and to find the best in us.

Winter brings diamonds under the soles of your feet.
Wait. Wait for the diamonds.
Imagine those glistening flakes winking at you, calling you to play.
Winter dusts your soul with joy.

Winter is a fine time to reflect and set intentions. It's not a time to feel blue, but to find peace. Use this tranquility as a tool to help move yourself and then your family into a beneficial rhythm.

The stark bareness of Winter strongly affects the human psyche. Research has revealed that extreme weather variance can negatively impact mental health negatively. When it's exceptionally cold, we tend to hunker down indoors a lot more, and so normal activities fall by the wayside. What could be called the "human hibernation syndrome" can amplify depression.[2]

Winter's shorter days and limited sunshine cause our bodies to produce more melatonin than in other seasons, as well as less serotonin. This automatically triggers a response: the neurotransmitter associated with happiness decreases significantly, whereas the chemicals produced that are linked to sleepiness and depression increase.

Being mindful of and preparing for the ways Winter may impact your mental health are great ideas. This might mean reaching out more to friends and family to maintain connection throughout the season. Sticking to some form of daily exercise and eating healthily will help keep your mood up and the endorphins flowing.

---

2. The Kim Foundation. "Winter Weather and Mental Health." Thekimfoundation.org. February 21, 2019. https://thekimfoundation.org/winter-weather-and-mental-health/#:~:text=With%20winter%20days%20being%20shorter,depression%20and%20sleepiness%20is%20increased.

Should you find yourself drifting down into depression, experiencing appetite or weight changes, missing work or school, and unable to enjoy activities, please consider seeking professional counseling.[3] Mood swings should be expected at certain levels due to extreme cold, snow, and similar conditions, but if you start having severe changes, be proactive and take action immediately. Remember, the cold weather will inevitably change, so focus on what you can control, like what you do want rather than what you do not, and take the best care of yourself possible on all levels.[4]

In our culture of unstoppable progress, any suggestion to slow down and reflect might be met with resistance. It shouldn't. Linearity is a human construct, negated by the reality of the natural world around us. Taking a break from continuous striving is not failure, on the contrary, it's the most effective course of action.

Winter is the time to find a cadence. It is a season to rejoice, to unwind by disconnecting from work, and to tap into the holiday festivities with our loved ones. It's an excellent time to organize and focus on what needs to be accomplished in the months ahead. Winter can be used as a tool to create new opportunities for those who seek them.

Winter is also a perfect time to stand out as a leader who inspires the troops and gets the work done swiftly. The season is often symbolized by an old, wise man—that's no coincidence. Winter can be a season of wisdom if you allow it to teach you its secrets. Why not give this a try rather than despairing about its idle, quiet cadence? Embrace it and use it to your advantage!

Nature rests during winter, waiting out the snow and the cold,

3. Ibid.
4. Ibid.

biding its time to act when the time comes. It's a chance to narrow down your choices and plan your actions.

As the saying goes:

> If you fail to plan, you are planning to fail.
>
> — BENJAMIN FRANKLIN

If you take on too much, which many do, you will very likely find yourself spinning out of control. Lean into your chosen community and bide your time. Spring is just around the corner.

> "Winter is coming."
>
> — GEORGE R.R. MARTIN, *A GAME OF THRONES*

Winter Prayer
Corinthians 13:11

Finally, brothers and sisters rejoice. Strive for full restoration, encourage one another, be of one mind, live in peace.

This calls for unity and actively working toward restoration and peace within the community.

My Memories of Winter

Babies

Well, I did the math and figured I was totally not gonna make it happen. I wanted at least two children, and I didn't have a boyfriend or anyone even on the horizon. I had many men interested, and I would go on dates. I figured at this point in time, it was simply a numbers game.

52 Saturdays in my 32nd year of life. I needed to maximize my odds of finding someone reasonable. When I met Michael, I was also dating several other prospects. I dropped them all. He was the one: brilliant, handsome, and from an exceptional family. Or so I thought. I started dating him seriously when I was 33, and we married when I was 35. Robbie, my first son, was born when I was 36, and Cash, my second son, was born when I was 39. I just barely made it happen. My husband walked out when Cash was 2 months old; I was not yet 40.

I crammed a lot into that very fast decade.

When I was engaged to be married, Michael told me to get a real steady job, a job for life. So I did. I was the manager of engineering and technology for OMAFRA, with the Province of Ontario. A very prestigious job with great benefits and a great salary. Life was good. I led the development of the green energy strategy for the province of Ontario and helped shape a new Economy. I completed the work while on bed rest, pregnant with Robbie.

I remember winning the crystal statue and getting a certificate for great vision and innovation. Yet none of it mattered really as I lay in the hospital at risk of losing my first child. The high-risk pregnancy unit suggested that I consider termination of the pregnancy. I was not well with toxemia or pre-eclampsia. My blood pressure was elevated. My legs and face, and arms were so swollen I was unrecognizable. I was terrified at times and yet also oddly at peace. Again, I am absolutely sure I was being carried. My husband was livid with me. He threw his wedding ring at me and walked out. This was the first time.

He said you can't shop for a doctor to tell you what you want to hear. I would sit still and calm and put my hands on my belly, and I would pray and calmly, peacefully, ask, 'Are you gonna be okay, little buddy?' I 100 percent, with every cell in my body, believed this baby would come and be perfect.

Robbie came a month early. My water broke all over the floor of Pino's salon. I had just gotten a pedicure and was about to get a manicure. I was wearing a beautiful black dress with my hair up, makeup on, and hoop earrings. Yes, I was as big as a house, although I tried that day to pretty myself up.

I called Michael and he picked me up, and wanted to take me straight to Grand River Hospital. I said no, I will take a cab to Toronto to Mount Sinai. The best hospital in Toronto is attached to sick kids. We fought. He drove me. He was livid.

Robbie came out purple as a plum. No crying. They worked on him. Then the doctor said to me Congratulations Susan, you would not have had this baby any other way. You made all the right decisions. My husband left and would not come home. So I joined him in Fort McMurray. I obtained the most prestigious position of Deputy CAO at the Regional Municipality of Wood Buffalo. My jurisdiction included all of the oil sands in Alberta, Canada. Robbie was 10 months old when I arrived.

I became pregnant again with twins in 2009, during the Great Recession. It was stressful to say the least. Robbie and I, along with the pregnancy, all returned to Waterloo. Michael did not follow.

So for my 2nd go-around with Cash, I followed my judgment and trusted my instincts. I hemorrhaged and lost one twin and got to keep Cash. It was all too much for Michael. Especially once Cash was diagnosed with a heart condition. That was the last doctor appointment Michael attended with me. I got to keep both Robbie and Cash, not the husband.

Pregnant, worked, pregnant, loss, grief, worked again.

Family

Set up the rhythm for the rest of the year as you launch into the festive season. This is one of my most timeless lessons, one that has helped me evolve beyond who I was. But it only came to fruition as an essential element of my year when I accepted my roots and who I started out as. By keeping the best and leaving the worst behind, I entered the next calendar year and the entire arena of life equipped with this most important of lessons.

A Season to be Celebrated with Family: Setting Up the Rhythm for the Year

Family traditions during winter, particularly around Christmas, play a crucial role in establishing family rhythms and setting the tone for the year ahead. These traditions, often passed down through generations, blend cultural influences and create a unique family identity. In this case, a mix of Ukrainian and Polish traditions highlights how each side of the family contributes different values and customs.

Baba is my grandmother on my father's side. She instilled important life rules and holiday traditions. She emphasized the importance of observing religious and ethnic holidays, particularly during the winter season from December 23rd to January 8th.

Baba insisted on following Ukrainian Christmas traditions, which included:

1. Preparing for the holiday season well in advance
2. Observing a "No Fly Zone" of celebration from December 23rd to January 8th
3. Attending the Ukrainian Christmas dinner on January 7th
4. Arriving before the first star appears in the sky on Christmas Eve

These traditions contrasted with those of my Polish grandmother on my mother's side, who focused on etiquette and perfection.

Key Polish Christmas traditions include the significant Christmas Eve celebration known as Wigilia (Polish pronunciation: [viˈɡilʲa], which involves extensive preparation, cooking, cleaning, and decorating. The meal features 12 dishes symbolizing the apostles and the months, along with the breaking of oplatek (Christmas wafers), the exchange of wishes, and the singing of many carols.

You may find an open seat at the Polish Christmas table, which is kept open for travelers or relatives. Poles felt nobody should be alone on the holiday, so they made it a habit to invite solo friends or neighbors.

Baba's insistence on honoring traditions, even when faced with work commitments, instilled a sense of rhythm and importance to the holiday season. She emphasized slowing down, calming down, and avoiding chaos during this period.

Baba's emphasis on Christmas traditions reminded me of a scene from "A Christmas Carol," where Fezziwig, a kind employer, demonstrates the importance of enriching people's lives through holiday celebrations.

Overall, Baba's teachings underscore the importance of

preserving cultural traditions and maintaining balance between work and festive observances.

The Setting of Family Goals

Every December, I buy a new notebook to plan my goals for the year. I divide it into sections for work, my kids, and other important people in my life. For each person, I write down big dreams and smaller steps to reach them. Even if a goal seems impossible, like fixing my son Cash's eyesight when doctors said it couldn't be done, I keep it on the list. By writing things down and thinking about them often, I believe we can make them happen.

I also set goals for my home and personal growth. When I talk to my family, I ask them what they want to achieve and help them think big.

The key is to be specific about what you want and keep working towards it, even if it takes years. It's important to think about all parts of your life - your mind, body, feelings, and surroundings. I use winter as a time to learn new things and grow as a family. By setting achievable goals and taking small steps, we can make big changes over time.

Every year, I put "Restore His Eyesight" at the top of Cash's goal list, even though doctors said it was impossible. After five years of trying different doctors and therapists, Cash's eyesight was miraculously restored!

Cash was blind and really behind in school. He couldn't read or write, even in 8th grade. I looked everywhere for help and finally found an awesome tutor named Katlyn, who also happened to be on Canada's National Boxing Team.

Katlyn didn't start with schoolwork right away. She worked on Cash's confidence first, which made a huge difference. She assigned him tasks he could perform well, gradually increasing their difficulty without informing him of the grade levels.

In just two years, Cash progressed from a pre-kindergarten level to nearly catching up to 6th grade. He's now only one year behind his classmates.

I also set other goals for Cash, like improving his body, mind, and spirit. We added fun activities like drives in the countryside, where he takes pictures and makes videos.

Cash and I have had long talks about how his learning journey will be different from others and that he is a superstar in his own way. Cash has focused on micro learning.

This whole experience taught me that writing down goals and working towards them can lead to amazing results, even when they seem impossible at first.

When you're making your goal lists, you have to think about what's driving you. For me, it was always the idea of wolves at the door. Lately, I'm not as concerned with the wolves at the door because they're just not coming anymore. But my point is that somebody else will have a different driver. What's your fear? Maybe you're afraid of stagnating.

Stay open to whatever the solution or realization of any goal may be. You must actively continue to probe, ask, seek, and listen. Then you formulate the solution. Be specific in setting these goals; ensure that you have your health in order, your head in order, your heart in order, and your home in order. I don't think most people approach this with sufficient intention. Subsequently, they wonder why their lives are out of control.

Or they think, "It's been a problem for years. I can't solve it." However, you haven't placed it on the list as a goal. That's the key. It took me years to get Cash's vision in order, but we worked at it and worked at it, and we continue to work at it. The point is, we've advanced.

Year after year, business leaders look at their finances. They may say something along the lines of, "This is not ideal, but some improvements have been made." Year after year, I would look at Cash's vision and say to him, "Your vision's not restored, but we've definitely moved the needle."

Head, heart, health, home. You have to address all aspects of your whole self.

I think of Winter as a time to develop new skills, learn things, and improve my family in general. How do I accomplish this? There are many ways to go about this. For instance, we do all kinds of things like nature walks, share moments of nothingness, notice nature and point it out.

Ask each of your family members to develop three personal development goals – small or big – and three family goals as a family unit. For example, "When Spring blossoms, where do we want to be as a person or family?" The goal can be grand, the steps to get there incremental.

The goals should not be too lofty. They must be achievable so that you can walk your way to success easily. I always say; baby steps. The next thing you know, you get there. Success.

Work

By now, I'm sure you understand what I mean when I say that Winter is a time for reflection, for stepping back, for observing your life. I've suggested ways that you can work on yourself and your family. But how can you apply Winter's tempo and opportunities to your work?

Remember: Winter is not a bountiful season—you will often feel pressed.

So what do you do when times are lean, and choices are few?

> "In seed time, learn; in harvest, teach, and in winter, enjoy."
>
> — WILLIAM BLAKE

Speeding Up by Slowing Down

The cadence proceeds as follows: *Restore, renew.*

Ask yourself, "What's working and/or not working for me, my work, my family, my community. What can I do better or differently? What should I stop? What should I start with? What should I continue?"

I do this every season. It's a great chance to stop something before it drains us of resources. You need to do this at least once a year—a five-year plan, for example, might be too late.

People want to be strategic and change their lives. I believe the best way to start doing this is by taking small steps that cumulatively will bring about a big change. That's what Winter's seasonal cadence allows us to create. The next season it can be another new thing or more of the same. It's the cumulative impact that makes great things happen.

The beginning of any journey that will change or improve your life is the most difficult. It includes the areas of family, friends, self-care, and work. Many people don't know how to proceed with this, and often struggle to begin the process. For example, if you get in your car, go onto the highway, but then go 100 miles the wrong way, you don't get where you want to go. In fact, you are double the distance away from your starting point and nowhere near where you wanted to go.

The heart of the secret is a paradox: it's all about *slowing down in order to speed up.*

Wolves at the Door

Being poor is like having "wolves at the door" - it means you're in a tough spot with few choices. Growing up poor taught me to always say "yes" to chances, work hard, and be thankful. When money is tight, it can feel frightening, but you can get through it. Sometimes, even successful people face money problems. And sometimes those problems are much bigger than my past poor problems. Both feel terrible.

The key is to stay calm and wait it out. In business, when people make weird choices, it might be because they're struggling with money. To escape poverty, try changing your surroundings, hanging out with different people, and working hard to improve your situation. Not everyone knows what it's like to be really broke, but those who do, understand how tough it can be. The good news is, with effort and smart choices, you can outrun those "wolves" and build a better life.

Winter is the season of slowing down. It's also the season of wolves. But what do you do when wolves come snarling and clawing at the door?

Some people don't know what it feels like to have "wolves at the door". It describes when you are left without choices, without time. The "wolves" are nipping at your heels, pressing you to the corner. Fear and pressure are making all the decisions for you. In such times, it doesn't matter what you want.

Growing up poor leaves a mark on you. I didn't want that for my kids, so I did my best to escape the "wolves". You can do that too.

You don't have many choices when you are broke. Very often in my life, I have lived with the "wolves" scratching at my door. This is why I have worn my poverty like a badge of honor. I understand all too well what little choices feel like, and urgent decisions are now critical and can make the difference between winning and losing everything. When I'm broke, I have no options, no safety net, and no opportunities. I must keep going. One foot in front of the other. I make a plan, I pray, I focus on positives, I feel what success would feel like, I imagine the best outcome, I work to surround myself with greatness.

I emphasize three main strategies for dealing with financial hardship, which I call "Wolves at the Door."

First, I advise always saying "yes" to reasonable opportunities, as this can lead to unexpected positive outcomes. I suggest leaving environments of poverty and seeking places with more opportunities, successful people and positive environments.

Second, when facing financial difficulties, I recommend staying steady and waiting it out, knowing that these challenges often pass.

Third, I stress the importance of recognizing desperate situations in business. I've noticed that people make different, often illogical decisions when under financial pressure. I advise looking more closely when observing unusual business decisions, as these may be signs of financial distress. Drawing from my personal experience, I've learned that being aware of these signs can help me identify and address financial issues quickly, both in my personal life and in business settings.

1. Always say 'yes' to new opportunities that may change your circumstances for the better. Assess the risk, take chances, try to open up new opportunities.

I live by the Butterfly Effect: Always say "Yes," in reasonable situations because you never know what new opportunities your choice will bring with it. If you don't say, "Yes," you'll never know what could have panned out from a missed chance. I always say yes to every opportunity that comes, and work like my life depends on it. I am thankful for what I have, yet it never seems to be enough.

God will help you rise up out of poverty. Seek, and you shall find. Remember, God helps those who help themselves.

Being broke sucks. Being ignorant sucks. If you are surrounded by poverty and ignorance, leave. Simply pick up and leave. Go to the land of opportunity. Go where intelligent people go. Go where people with money go. Eventually, the smart money will rub off on you. Provided you study and work as though your life depends on it (because it does!). Adjust your mindset. Focus on positives. Believe in success.

2. Wait it Out and Keep Steady.

I have been very successful in my career, and I have made money. Yet from time to time, the "wolves" return to the door. I am now okay with the "wolves" when they show up, because I know it is not me they are looking for.

When they are at the door, it's a familiar feeling. I just wait them out, keep steady, and sometimes move slightly to the left or to the right. They eventually go away. I know the "wolves" are not looking for me anymore.

3. Recognise a Desperate Situation and Get Ahead of it.

Remember this: people make very different decisions when the "wolves" are at the door. If you are talking to someone or observing something weird in business, like illogical decisions, take a moment to see if these decisions were made because of the "wolves".

In business, when I see decisions or choices made that don't seem the best or ideal, I dig a bit deeper and say to myself, 'Aahhh, this is a familiar move; looks like they made this decision because the "wolves" are at the door.' Being broke is being broke; even in ivory towers. On several occasions, I found myself working with a project or a company in serious financial trouble. Broke looks and smells the same everywhere. Desperate times, desperate measures.

Choices, time, and opportunities typically lead to sound decisions. Sure, when you can make the best decisions, guess what? You usually make good decisions. But when the "wolves" are at the door, you make what seems like odd decisions. Decisions made under pressure are less comprehensive and rational.

Being broke is not openly talked about in business. You have to know the signs. This is not something people talk about, because who the hell wants the "wolves" at their door? Lucky for me, my history with, and mindfulness of the damn wolves, have helped me to be able to sniff out broken activities and get in front of them fast.

4. Change Your Environment.

Change your attitude, interact with different people, change your environment, and run fast. Outsmart and outrun the "wolves". If you succeed in doing so, they will eventually leave you alone altogether. Some people don't even know what it is like to have the "wolves" at the door. Lucky them! But ask anyone who has ever struggled, past or present, and they will have a story about those "wolves".

Winter is the time to lead with your example. It's time to be successful and effective. The preseason, if you will, is a time of profound reading and learning. Naturally, everybody is getting into the holiday spirit.

How to Think Like a C-Suite Person

As a C-Suite leader, it's crucial to conduct yourself professionally, especially as the year ends.

How to prepare: Reverse engineer your goals, assessing what needs to be done at work and home before December 23rd.

When you're setting goals, you need to think backwards from what you want to achieve.

Look at what needs to be done at work and home before the holidays start. Ask yourself questions like, "How can I get everything ready by December 23rd? What do I need to do to start the New Year right?"

It's important to keep things running smoothly, like steering a ship with the wind in its sails. You should check in with colleagues, ensure projects are on track, and help everyone feel calm and prepared. This kind of leadership makes you look really professional, even if you don't have a fancy job title yet. It's not just about being a boss - it's about showing you can handle things well, no matter what time of year it is. This approach works for everyone, from new employees to experienced managers. The main idea is to stay calm, be ready for anything, and help your team feel confident and prepared.

How to lead effectively: Maintain a calm, steady hand while driven by a sense of urgency. Pace yourself through each season, providing consistent guidance and support.

To be seen as a great leader, act like one, especially as the year ends. By December 23rd, you should have everything under control. Check in with your colleagues, ensure projects are on track, and help everyone feel calm.

This makes you look super professional, even if you're not the boss yet. Good leaders stay calm but work with urgency, whether they're in charge already or working their way up. This approach works for everyone, from new employees to experienced managers. It's all about making your workplace steady and showing you can handle anything. Remember, it's not just about being the boss - it's about being someone people trust and respect, no matter what time of year it is.

How to handle issues: Address problems head-on, working with your team to resolve them before the holidays.

How to create a work rhythm: Lean into the cadence of the season, allowing for a period of slowing down and reflection around the Winter Solstice.

How to delegate: Identify tasks that only you can do as a leader, and delegate the rest without abdicating responsibility.

How to build trust: Be consistent, avoid being an alarmist, and create a natural cadence within the season.

How to connect with your team: Share your vision, tie your work to personal commitments, and show that you care about the community. By following these principles, you'll establish yourself as a trusted leader, capable of guiding your team through the end-of-year period and into the new year with confidence and clarity.

Pace yourself.

As a leader, you need to keep a steady pace throughout the year, just like the changing seasons. Your role is to guide and support your team, regardless of what happens. If problems arise, address them directly. Tell your team, "We'll work together through tough times and celebrate good times." Try to fix issues before the holidays, even if you can't solve everything.

Make a plan to address any remaining problems in January. This way, everyone can relax during their break. People will trust you more if they know you've got things under control. It's like when I had to make sure work was done before going to my grandma's for Christmas dinner - I didn't want any problems interrupting family time. When you handle things this way, your team will think, "Our leader's got this. We can trust them."

Be consistent.

As a leader, it's important to stay calm and not panic, especially around the holidays. Everyone's looking forward to winter break and the New Year, so try to keep things steady. Don't make major changes or panic during this time. Instead, find a way to work that fits with the season.

This might mean slowing down a bit as the year ends. People in charge, like company presidents and board members, really like it when leaders do this. It helps everyone feel less stressed and more confident in their leader. Your colleagues will appreciate it as well, because they also need time to relax, think, and prepare for the new year. When you stay calm and confident, it helps your whole team feel better and trust you more.

Lean into the cadence of the season.

I've also found that adopting a seasonal cadence significantly helped my teams. We created a "can-do" sprint. We were empowered and aware, with a steady commitment to taking action when needed and to slowing down to speed up. This is an extremely useful skill during the cold, long days that come with the Winter season.

I've been operating with cadence and confidence for at least 20 years, doing this in the C-suite, sometimes even without announcing exactly what I'm doing. If you're going to lead and want to emulate this model, make sure to give yourself a break come December 23rd. At that point, take your foot off the gas. Fashion your efforts around this idea of the Winter Solstice. Share with those with whom you work: "When we get to the shortest day, we're going to take our foot off the gas."

Trust the rhythm.

Being a good leader is like following the beat in a song, like Paul Simon's "Diamonds on the Soles of Her Shoes." Just as the song has a catchy rhythm that makes you want to dance, good leadership has a natural flow that people want to follow. In the song, Paul Simon combines different musical styles to create something new and exciting. As a leader, you can mix different ideas and ways of doing things to make your team work better.

The song starts slow and builds up, just like how you might start a new project slowly and then pick up the pace. The lyrics discuss walking with diamonds on your shoes, which could suggest walking with confidence. As a leader, you need to show confidence in your team and your plans. When you trust the natural rhythm of leadership, such as following the beat of a great song, your team will want to follow you and work together more effectively.

> Whether you're a business owner or a leader, new people join your team. They join with a cadence already established. They've got something inside of them that yearns for this. You find that, if you do this year by year, you can expect it to improve for the company.

Delegate, But Don't Abdicate

As a leader, it's important to plan ahead and share tasks with your team. This is called delegating. But you can't give away all your work - that's called abdicating. You need to determine which tasks only you can do as the leader. For example, reading a bedtime story to your kids is something you should do yourself, not ask someone else to do.

At work, there are tasks that show you're in charge, like leading important meetings or cutting ribbons at events. Make a list of these important jobs that only you should do. This helps people see you as a real leader. It's also good to show that you care about your work and your community. Like when I walked around my hometown with my kids, it showed people that I really cared about the place, not just my job. When you do these things, it helps people trust you more as a leader.

THE 4 Hs (HEAD, HEART, HEALTH & HOME) - Braiding Family, Self, Work and Community Into One Whole

How to be a great leader during Winter:

Set goals that help your company, customers, team, and yourself. Make sure you can measure your success by Spring. To get your team excited about a goal, make sure it's smart and touches their hearts. Think about how your work can make people's lives better and healthier. When setting goals, do a quick check: Does it fit at least two of these - head, heart, health, or home? Don't forget to set goals with your family, too.

How to build confidence and transform your community:

Believe in yourself, even when others doubt you. Take breaks to let your mind rest and generate new ideas. Don't be afraid to tackle big problems, like improving schools in your community. Work with others and keep pushing until you succeed.

How to create a better work environment:

Pay attention to the spaces where people work and take breaks. Make sure they're clean, comfortable, and have everything people need. This shows your team that they matter. The same goes for your home and town - fixing up these places can make everyone feel better and work harder.

How to make spaces special:

Be real and create rituals that work both at home and at work. It's not about spending money, but about marking important moments. When planning events, consider small details such as where people sit. These things might seem small, but they can make people feel valued and happy.

Remember, as a leader, you can make Winter a positive time by planning ahead, believing in yourself, taking care of your team, and making spaces special. This can help everyone work better and feel more connected.

Goals set as a leader should advance the company, the customer's business, the team, and your career path. These goals should yield measurable results by the end of Winter, serving as a springboard for future options.

'You should have measurable success', it's part of an endless loop in my head, *'heart, health, and home'*. I have to loop that in to become a better solution provider and leader.

To ignite a team, the goal must make sense to them even if they decide, *maybe this could work.'* It's got to be smart enough so they can see, *'Oh, that could work.'*

Goals should also resonate with the heart, evoking empathy and care. When establishing new schools, I emphasized community benefits. *'It would be great not only for my kids, but more importantly, for so many others.'*

The condition of a school impacts students' self-worth. When children enter a broken-down, ramshackle school, they internalize its condition. If the school isn't worth repairing or cleaning, they may think their education isn't worth it either, and, further, that they themselves lack value.

Social causes should promote health and sustainability, benefiting not just those directly involved but also their broader networks.

I use a "head, heart, health, home" checklist for goal-setting, aiming to advance causes by the end of Winter. This approach extends to family life: *"Robbie, what do you want to accomplish this Winter? What's important to you? What do you think would help your situation in whatever way?"*

This tactical approach is crucial; you've got the cadence down, and then you've got to establish the what. Next comes the how? How do I do this? That is important. Why are you doing this? What is your why?

Community

My journey through the seasons has taught me a key lesson: everything is interconnected. Anything I do at home or at work eventually radiates into my community. If I strive to achieve the best for my family, and then for my career and business, my community will be all the richer for it, in one way or another. This realization has become the bedrock of my life and of my actions—another natural law to live by.

Self-Confidence is the Magic Pill

Sometimes in our lives, we come across problems that seem insurmountable. Usually, the all-encompassing ones involve not just your home and your work, but the world at large. How to tackle these problems when it seems that everyone who came before you failed.

Well, if you're ever going to build a stronger community around you, you have to first become stronger yourself. You have to believe in yourself, and that self-confidence will be the magic that will transform the world.

> I transformed my community by believing in myself.

> Family, work, and community are never separate.

This is a lesson in setting a goal and then being the right leader, one that takes lessons from their environment and knows a great idea when they hear one.

As a strong leader, there's a considerable element of confidence that you must exhibit to build trust. Typically, when people enter Winter, it's essentially a negative experience. But when you prepare for it in advance, you can make the most of Winter and leverage it to your advantage.

Natural Laws of Winter

Winter is a special time for looking inward. It's as if nature is giving you a quiet moment to reflect on what you truly want in life and to rest your body and mind. Use this time to understand yourself better and recharge.

During winter, it's important to be careful with your energy and time. Just like animals have to be smart about using their resources in the cold months, you should think carefully before taking on new tasks. Instead, focus on taking care of yourself and others, especially since some people might feel extra sad during this time of year.

Winter, often perceived as a time of dormancy, actually presents unique opportunities for personal growth and preparation. This season embodies several natural laws that can guide us towards self-improvement and efficient living. The quietude of winter serves as a canvas for clarity, allowing us to discern our true desires and sources of happiness more easily.

Much like a snow-covered landscape helps important features stand out, winter's stillness can illuminate what truly matters in our lives. This period also demands efficiency, as limited resources require us to optimize our strengths and make the most of what we have, mirroring nature's remarkable ability to thrive with minimal means.

Self-reflection becomes paramount during winter, offering us a rare chance to simply "be" and understand ourselves better. It's a time for restoration, focusing on rest and inner rejuvenation. However, this season also calls for caution and care. It's crucial to be discerning about new commitments, setting budgets and workloads in advance to allow for a winter "autopilot" mode.

Moreover, winter, especially during the holiday season, requires heightened vigilance about mental health - both our own and that of our loved ones. By embracing these natural laws of winter - opportunity, efficiency, self-reflection, restoration, and mindful care - we can use this season as a powerful tool for personal growth, preparing ourselves for the renewal and activity of the coming spring.

Winter, particularly the Christmas season, plays a crucial role in establishing family rhythms and traditions that can shape the entire year. This section explores a rich array of cultural practices, primarily drawing on Ukrainian and Polish heritage passed down through generations. My experiences, influenced by both my Baba (grandmother) and my Polish side of the family, highlight the diversity and importance of these traditions.

The winter season, as observed in the Ukrainian tradition, extends from December 23 to January 8 and is characterized by preparation, celebration, and reflection. It emphasizes the need to create a "No Fly Zone" for festivities, even amidst busy work schedules. Polish Christmas traditions are also detailed, including the significance of Christmas Eve (Wigilia), the preparation of 12 symbolic dishes, and the practice of breaking oplatek (Christmas wafers) while exchanging wishes. The importance of attending midnight mass (Pasterka) is also noted.

These family traditions serve as more than just annual rituals; they offer valuable life lessons about balancing work and personal life, renewing hope and optimism, and respecting cultural heritage while adapting to modern life. The text draws parallels between these family practices and business leadership, using the example of Fezziwig from "A Christmas Carol" to illustrate how traditions and celebrations can enrich people's lives beyond the workplace.

Ultimately, this section underscores the importance of maintaining family traditions as a means of establishing a positive rhythm throughout the year. It encourages readers to embrace their cultural heritage, prepare thoughtfully for the holiday season, and use this time to foster connections and renewal, both in personal and professional spheres.

Winter is a special time for opportunities and self-discovery. Just like it's easier to see things in a snowy landscape, the quiet of winter helps us understand what makes us happy. It's also a time to be smart with our energy, like animals in nature who make the most of what they have. Winter provides an opportunity to reflect on who we are and what we want in life.

Winter is perfect for resting and healing. It's different from summer, when we're busy filling ourselves up with activities. In winter, we should give our body, mind, and heart a break. It's not a time to be hard on ourselves, but to listen carefully to what we need. If we pay attention, we might notice little signs or feelings that tell us something important about ourselves.

During winter, it's best to take it easy and not plan too much. Be careful about adding new tasks. Instead, use this time to rest and think deeply. It's smart to have your plans and work set up in the fall, so in winter you can relax and go with the flow.

Opportunity

Winter is the time of opportunities. Just like a snow-covered landscape makes it easier for things to stand out, so does the time of quiet help you realize what it is you want in life. It makes it easier to see what makes you happy. Grab that opportunity, as the rabbit grabs at any morsel of food they come across.

Efficiency

During the lean times of winter, you will have to utilize your strengths to the best effect. Nothing should go to waste… You just don't have the luxury. Nature is amazing at doing the most with the least; there are plenty of lessons to get from that. To be efficient, you must also *know who you are*, which brings us to the next natural law.

Self-reflection

Humans are the only animals that don't simply "be"; we analyze, reflect and constantly search for our place in life. Other animals have the advantage of knowing precisely who they are and where they are supposed to be going, simply by existing. They know what they need to do at any given point in order to survive. We, on the other hand, have to take the extra step and figure it out by ourselves. Winter is the perfect moment to just "be."

Restoration and Restorative

We must note that Summer also embodies restoration. Granted, restoration in Summer is different than Winter's version, but it's still a restorative period. The restorative period in Winter encompasses a sense of hibernation, whereas in the Summer, restoration is about filling oneself.

In the wintertime, it's truly about giving your body a break, giving your mind a break, giving your heart a break. Winter is not a time to be hard on yourself. Winter is really a time to listen, to rest, restore, reflect, and to listen carefully to the rhythm of your own mind, body, and soul.

In Winter, if you don't do that, you're going to miss cues, little messages. It's like when your body or mind becomes symptomatic. Many times in the Winter, I'll think, "That's interesting. Why am I reacting like that?" Well, there's usually a symptom. Symptoms are good because they alert you to the fact that there's something you need to further explore.

Wintertime should be about deep reflection and a lot of rest. Resist the temptation to engage in excessive socializing. In the Fall, you book your calendar with projects. In the Winter months, though, it's best to be very careful and discerning. When any new initiative comes to you, think long and hard about whether you want to add that to your plate.

When you do that, even if it can fit, there's a really good chance that you've not given yourself enough time to rest or restore. That's why budgets and workloads should be set in the Fall so that in Winter, you're on autopilot.

Suicide Rates During Winter

Contrary to popular belief, New Year's Day, not Christmas, marks the peak for suicide rates. This sobering statistic underscores the complex interplay of factors contributing to suicide risk during the winter season. Depression, the "contagion effect" from awareness of other suicides, and desperation stemming from failed relationships, financial difficulties, or fear of public humiliation all play significant roles in this heightened risk.[5]

Given these realities, it's crucial to remain vigilant about your own mental health and that of your loved ones during the winter months, particularly around the holidays and New Year's Day[6] Be attentive to signs of distress, such as unusual isolation or withdrawal from everyday activities. Offer support by listening without judgment and encourage professional help when needed. Remember, your care and attention could be lifesaving, costing nothing more than your time and compassion.

I share this information just to let you know: In Winter, and particularly at the holidays and New Year's Day especially, please stay vigilant about how you yourself are feeling, and stay in close touch with your loved ones who may have been silently displaying a call for help, such as isolating more than usual, not returning calls or participating in events.

Do your best to steer them toward excellent professional help, and let them know that you're available to listen anytime they feel like they need support. It could save a life, and it doesn't cost you anything other than taking the time to care and be someone they can vent to and be completely honest with.

Tips for the Season: Embracing Winter's Tranquility

At the start of Winter, you will be better able to stay focused with a clear list of achievable goals for work, home, and family. Develop an executable plan, involving your team in the process.

---

5. Degges-White, Ph.D., Suzanne. "Suicide Risk Spikes After the Holidays." Psychology Today. December 6, 2018. https://www.psychologytoday.com/us/blog/lifetime-connections/201812/suicide-risk-spikes-after-the-holidays
6. Degges-White, Ph.D., Suzanne. "Suicide Risk Spikes After the Holidays." Psychology Today. December 6, 2018. https://www.psychologytoday.com/us/blog/lifetime-connections/201812/suicide-risk-spikes-after-the-holidays

Delegate tasks while monitoring progress towards your goals. Regularly reflect and reassess.

If new opportunities arise, be prepared to adjust your plan, declining some commitments or acquiring additional resources as needed. Remember, Winter is a restorative period, so balance is crucial.

This applies to family life too. Establish rhythms for rest and connection. For example, choose a Netflix series to watch with your child or pick a theme for documentaries to enjoy together. These intentional decisions create shared experiences and memories.

For busy professionals, it's important to practice being present without distractions. Winter offers holidays and celebrations, but also provides time for restoration, rest, and reflection. By following these steps, you can make the most of the season both professionally and personally.

Case Study: Check Yourself Before You Wreck Yourself - Helping Jane

I was fortunate enough to land a huge coaching assignment. I was really excited and nervous to take on the assignment, because it was the height of the COVID-19 pandemic. Much was at stake for the client and for me.

Yes, struggling with impostor syndrome, I took on the assignment. I started with a fabulous exercise of digging into gaining a good understanding of the lay of the land. I met with the three bosses together, and then one by one I asked; What has been done so far? What is working well? What is not working? What is getting in the way? And, what is at stake?

Essentially, I performed a very basic SWOT analysis disguised by simple 15-minute one-to-ones. The client identified a wonderful trajectory to rise in the ranks of the company. They had invested heavily in this leader, and she stalled out. Plateau. Well, actually worse. She was on the brink of being fired, or best, best-case scenario, simply continuing to be a part of the company, but at a huge risk of not advancing. Morale was in the garbage.

The bosses chose me to help. At first, I thought, 'What on Earth could I possibly do to help?'

I clung to the process. I studied and focused on the process. Stakeholders. Check. One-to-one. Check. Goal. Check.

Now I had to engage and win over the languishing leader. A beautiful, super successful, ultra competitive leader who had absolutely everything going for her. I started with a one-hour discovery session with Jane. She was lovely. We hit it off right away. She was a winner all around. She kept getting passed over for promotions. Other than that, she won at everything she did. Additionally, some of her colleagues disliked her. She was a superstar, an overachiever, and she was fabulous.

I could see her passion, her energy, and her focus. She was always stepping up and taking the bull by the horns.

So, what was the problem? Jane missed one fundamental job. In fact, she missed the top priority. Her main job. She did not fully recognize that it was her job to build her superstar team.

Whenever her team faced a significant problem or obstacle, she dug in, solved the problem, got it done, and moved on. She was an excellent problem solver and a workhorse.

Jane failed miserably at building a get-it-done team. Her team retention was in the toilet. Like a revolving door. She was constantly short-staffed. Always recruiting and training, and always with vacant positions.

She still got the outcomes so she didn't think it was a big deal. The world was in the midst of the COVID-19 pandemic, business was booming, and demand for products and services was massive. The bosses wanted to elevate Jane, but they could not figure out why she could not build and keep a team.

We began with what she thought was impeding her. Yes, there were tears and intense emotions about what more she could do.

I used the Marshall Goldsmith Stakeholder-Centered Coaching method, and it was effective. In fact, before we ended the process, Jane got two promotions, and the bosses asked how I did it. Well, we all did it together.

We assembled the stakeholders, direct reports, peers, and her bosses. We landed on a goal. Jane simply wanted to advance her leadership in a noticeable way whereby stakeholders could see changes in behavior that benefited her leadership and team.

I conducted one-on-one meetings with the stakeholders. Jane asked the stakeholders permission to participate. She asked them to be candid, kind, and specific about action and behaviour. Specifically, we asked what Jane could start, stop, and continue doing to become more like the leader they wanted and needed to be. I prepared a detailed report after the interviews.

I conducted weekly coaching with Jane over a 6-month period. 15-30 minutes maximum every week. The stakeholders also became involved, providing regular feedback. Jane also leaned in and solicited feedback from stakeholders in real time. Jane listened and took incremental steps, with specific actions and observable behavioral changes.

Here is the list:

- Stop eye rolling in meetings
- Start listening more and asking others for input and ideas.
- Stop doing everything herself.

We consulted stakeholders on an interim report. Yes, we were making progress. The stakeholders noticed a huge change.

What was observed:

In meetings, Jane would get red in the face, visibly frustrated by teammates. She would roll her eyes, and it would look like she was being dismissive to other ideas and suggestions, and even reacting this way to work submitted. She would appear impatient and she would be very direct in meetings. The appearance of collaboration and integrative thinking, teamwork and team input appeared to be minimized with one eye roll.

The super interesting part was that Jane had no idea she was so animated. She was unaware of the eye roll and other behaviors that were impeding her ability to ignite and build her team.

So we played a weekly game via video Zoom and we would play back the video, and very specifically, we made a mantra Check yourself before you wreck yourself.

Stop with the eye roll. Shut your damn mouth. Listen more, ask more. Meet people where they are at. Stop rescuing the team. Stop solving all the problems by yourself. Be intentional in team building. Ask the team to contribute. React with a positive, open frame of mind. Continue being a superstar; however, start showing vulnerability and openly acknowledge that you cannot do this alone.

Building Jane's team is her primary responsibility. The feedback from stakeholders provided Jane with the insight to make lasting, incremental behavioral changes. Stop, Start, Continue saved the day. Stakeholders working with leaders led to two promotions.

Jane literally enjoyed the process. Once she clearly identified the behaviours she needed to change, and with stakeholder feedback, she adjusted and won over her teammates.

She was an amazing, receptive, and coachable leader in the process, and she embraced the change.

Not at first though. At first she battled against change. Once she saw the eye roll on video and the visual cues she gave, with her cheeks flushed red, she realized she could not continue this way.

We talked about executive presence. She read books on integrative thinking and meeting teammates where they are at. She became a coach and mentor for her teammates; she showed more authentic aspects of herself and vulnerability. Her stakeholders embraced the change and committed to helping her become the leader she was meant to be. Teamwork makes the dreamwork.

Marshall Goldsmith recognizes 12 behaviours that women do that get in their own way. They are:

- **Reluctance to claim your achievements:** Downplaying accomplishments or talking about the team's success rather than one's specific role.
- **Expecting others to spontaneously notice and reward your contributions:** Assuming hard work will be recognized without explicitly highlighting results.
- **Overvaluing Expertise:** Focusing solely on building technical expertise rather than developing leadership skills and a broader network.
- **Building rather than leveraging relationships:** Excelling at creating strong personal relationships but being hesitant to use them for career advancement.

- **Failing to enlist allies from day one:** Waiting too long to build a network of supporters, mentors and sponsors.
- **Putting your job before your career:** Being highly loyal to a specific role's duties at the expense of investing time in long-term career growth.
- **The Perfection Trap:** Setting excessively high standards, which can make delegation difficult and lead to self-criticism.
- **The "disease to please":** An excessive desire for approval, which can lead to difficulty saying no or setting boundaries.
- **Minimizing:** Using language or physical behaviors that minimize one's presence or contributions.
- **Ruminating:** Overthinking or dwelling on past mistakes or negative interactions.
- **Letting your radar distract you:** Being overly attuned to the political environment and potential threats rather than focusing on goals and opportunities.

In Marshall Goldsmith's Stakeholder Centered Coaching Method, which I used to help Jane, he focuses on the following key principles;

- **Stakeholder-driven:** Success is defined by positive changes in stakeholders' perceptions, not by the leader's self-assessment.
- **Future-focused:** The process emphasizes letting go of the past and focusing on future improvement.
- **Focus on behaviour:** The method targets one or two key behaviours for improvement to ensure a practical and impactful outcome.
- **Integrated with work:** The coaching is integrated into the leader's daily work and interactions, rather than being a separate activity.

- **Parallel change:** Both the leader's behaviour and the stakeholder's perceptions are intended to change simultaneously.

The 7 Step Process

1. **Identify:** The leader chooses 1-2 specific behaviours to improve.
2. **Engage:** Stakeholders who are affected by these behaviours are involved in the process.
3. **Collect:** The leader gathers feedback from stakeholders to understand the current impact of their behaviours.
4. **Develop:** An action plan is created based on the feedback to address the desired change.
5. **Implement:** The leader implements the action plan and regularly performs the new behaviours.
6. **Check-In:** The leader periodically checks in with the stakeholders to assess progress and make adjustments.
7. **Continue:** Positive changes are maintained and new goals are set for ongoing development. [7]

Leadership Lesson for Winter

When you are feeling weak and trouble is all around you, stop and reflect as hard as you can to find moments of gratitude.

Questions to ask:

- What are you grateful for?
- What do you appreciate?
- What are you looking forward to?
- How do you ride the wave of uncertainty?

7. M. Goldsmith, personal communication, May 20, 2013

Lean in, take action, line up all the pieces and then release. Rinse and repeat. Keep it up until you are buoyant and riding the wave of uncertainty.

When you are drowning in negativity and cannot keep your head above water, sit back, relax, reflect, and literally ask yourself what is going on; why is this happening? You don't need to have clear answers, because the universe is working in your favor for so many reasons you do not understand.

Focus on persistence. Imagine success. Write down what you want. Be specific. State it as if it were true, as if it had already happened.

Trust the process. You are a very important part of the process. Note that sometimes it can be a very long game for you to recognize what and why something is happening. Manifestation is very powerful. Seek, and you shall find. Live and breathe success. Small and big successes are possible with a growth mindset.

Placemaking at the Heart of Everything

One of the things woven throughout this entire journey is the environment. When I say that, I don't mean Mother Nature. I mean placemaking and the space in which you function. The place in which you exist or where you're trying to work/succeed. This environment can suffocate you or make you soar.

> *Placemaking is the integration of design elements into everyday life. It ties back to the seasons. It also creates a part of the depth and, with how it comes the feeling that I'm leading and living a more prosperous life.*

I've worked hard at placemaking. Many employers/leaders will overlook these spaces where people take breaks. When you walk in there, and it looks and feels dreary, it tells me that the leadership thinks I'm not worth it. With every C-suite role I've held, the first thing I would do is enter with the intention of improving the organization. Placemaking.

Creating an environment that says, "You matter. You are my space, and you matter." When you go and break bread with your workmates, these are some of the most important times you share. That's when you're coming together. That's when your circadian rhythm changes. It's a restorative time and a time of rest.

From an architectural perspective, it affects people's perceptions. They oscillate at different frequencies. They're more creative, more inspired; they're excited to be there. I found that the moment you change the place or the space, you get much better work out of people.

The same applies to your home or your town. What did I do in Swift Current? The first thing I did was right the community by focusing on the heart of their town, the downtown. The downtown was broken. It looked ramshackle; it was in severe disrepair. Market Square and making the downtown beautiful was very important to me in Swift Current. Creating reasons to gather in beautiful spaces created with pride.

I think many C-suite people miss that.

You're going to make your team the absolute strongest when their space, the place that they're in, is comfortable. Do they have everything they need? Do they have the right tools? Ask them, "Are you happy? Great. I'm going to be calling upon you, and when I do, I need you to rise to the occasion." When you do, so will they.

When I walked into a particular lunchroom, it was dirty and broken. The couch was filthy, and the tables were gross. I've done this a million times. Even with the executives that I have coached, I'll go on a tour of their place, and I'll say, "First thing I'm going to do is give you a good tongue-lashing about the place." The front end looks good, but the back end is rotting. Ramshackle.

They ask, "What do you mean by that?"

I mean it's in disrepair, severe disrepair. I used to do dinner theater. You're selling these meals for $200 a pop; the place is packed, the people are eating and I'm coming out to do some singing and dancing. But I'm an entertainer. I must use the back parking lot and the back door when I enter the facility.

As I'd go through that kitchen, I'd be thinking, "Oh, my God. I would never eat here. There are bugs in the flour. Mold and mildew are growing in this corner." It's the same concept. The restaurants that do exceptionally well consistently have an excellent front end, a good middle, and an excellent back end.

As you're readying your plans, projects, and teams in Winter, you should also do some placemaking. It's essential. And Winter is when I like to do that.

Some suggestions for successful 'Placemaking':

1. *You must be vulnerable and authentic.* Find something that you can weave into your home life and work life. Otherwise, you're caught up in imposter syndrome, where you have two different worlds going on. You must choose to be authentic both at work and at home. It's the same.
2. *Create rituals. It's not about spending.* I grew up very poor. When I describe this, it's not about money. It's

> about making it special. Some companies or some people might say, "I don't have the money to do that." Again, it's not about money. It's about saying, "I'm going to mark the moment. We're going to be entering the Winter Solstice. I will mark the moment by reading my environment, my place, and my space. There are going to be a few traditions/rituals/practices/habits that I'm going to do." Intentions matter, and so do real actions. Even the smallest gesture can make a huge difference.

Some people put up Christmas decorations, but this time is really about readying your place. At my Baba's, we would set the table and underneath the tablecloth, we would put hay. It's not about spending tons of money; we just brought in the hay from outside. But we all knew the hay was there, and it symbolized the manger of baby Jesus.

These are examples of small steps you can take to prepare your space and to say, "We're entering into the Winter Solstice." We're readying our homes. We're readying our business."

I found that some of the wealthiest, most elaborate companies that I worked for felt the coldest and the least inviting, the least warm and creative. They wouldn't make sufficient effort at placemaking. They didn't go through the placemaking effort, and they didn't operate with integrity and love. Their heart wasn't in it.

I've gone to some fancy dinners where I would immediately feel, "God, get me out of here." On the other hand, I could attend a family dinner where they didn't have much money, but as soon as I arrived, it felt very rich. They valued me. When I walked in the door, they gave me their best linen, china, or cups. They had nothing compared to wealthy people, but they gave me their best.

Conversely, you can go to a fancy place and feel wholly disrespected because they didn't make any effort to value you, or make you feel special.

Here's an idea to try at your workplace:

Fun Fridays

Put a candy bar in the desk of a person on your team that you think was the leader of that week, somebody who went out of their way to do something special. Little things like this can turn into spirit-boosting rituals.

People miss this point. It's about high touch. It's about honoring human beings. Why do people perform better in a particular environment? Why do they feel so much love here versus where they used to work? How can you make spaces where everyone feels welcome? You can create these unique places. It's about ritual and tradition. It's about designing these spaces and rituals with intent.

When I host and create team efforts, people often tell me it looks effortless. I recall one time at Langdon Hall, where I organized a meeting for some key clients. We spent three days together. A lot of these women and men had never met.

I took particular care in setting the table, the seating arrangement, and its placement in the room. All of these little pieces matter. In the end, I could feel them all vibrating with joy. I had made an effort and it paid off. Being considerate and intentional.

When you enter Winter, you should say to yourself, "What can I do to elevate this place?" It's not just the team. What can you do with this place, what you're working with, to put something special on it? It could be a repositioning of a table. It could be traditions or rituals. Whatever it is, it becomes valuable because you value it as a leader. You said, "I'm going to make this special," and then, boom! It's special because you put some effort into it.

> "Winter is a season of recovery and preparation."
>
> — PAUL THEROUX

Winter Takeaways

Reflect–think of where you are in your life and where you want to be.

Winter blues aren't all bad. The cold season is a great time to slow down, reflect on your life, and make plans. Instead of feeling sad, use the quiet time to set goals and establish a good routine for your family.

Take care of yourself in winter. The cold and dark can make you feel down, so it's important to stay active, eat well, and keep in touch with friends and family. If you start feeling really sad or can't enjoy things, don't be afraid to ask for help from a doctor or counselor.

Rest–you need rest in order to come back in spring.

Restore–replenish and restore your mental and physical supplies.

> "Spring passes and one remembers one's innocence.
>
> Summer passes and one remembers one's exuberance.
>
> Autumn passes and one remembers one's reverence.
>
> Winter passes and one remembers one's perseverance."
>
> — YOKO ONO

Ancient Cultures and the Winter Solstice

Ancient cultures celebrated the Winter Solstice in many interesting ways. The Neolithic people, who lived around 10,200 BC, built special monuments, such as Newgrange in Ireland, to align with the sunrise on the shortest day of the year. They probably used these places for important rituals.

The Romans held a major festival called Saturnalia to honor their god of agriculture. Some Romans also celebrated the birthday of Mithra, a god of light, on December 25th.

In Scandinavia, people celebrated Yule by bringing home huge logs to burn for up to 12 days. They believed the sparks from these Yule logs would bring good luck for the new year. Here's how to celebrate like the ancient Norse:

1. Find a big log
2. Decorate it with pine cones or ribbons
3. Burn it in a fireplace, if you have one, or just pretend
4. Have a feast with your family and friends

The Incas in South America had a festival called Inti Raymi to honor their sun god. They would fast for three days, then gather to watch the sunrise and make special offerings.

In China, people celebrate Dong Zhi by eating special foods like colorful rice balls or dumplings. In Japan, people take baths with yuzu to promote good health in the new year.

Native American tribes like the Zuni and Hopi have their own traditions. The Zuni perform a special dance called Shalako, while the Hopi celebrate with an all-night ceremony called Soyal. Both involve special leaders who announce the exact moment of the solstice.

These ancient traditions demonstrate how important the changing seasons were to people worldwide. Many of us still celebrate the Winter Solstice today, carrying on these old customs in new ways.

> "In the depth of winter, I finally learned that there was in me an invincible summer."
>
> — ALBERT CAMUS

> "They who sing through the summer must dance in the winter."
>
> — ITALIAN PROVERB

Winter Solstice's Spiritual Significance

Everything lies dormant in the silent earth in Winter.[8] It's a time to rest and reflect in anticipation of Spring's awakening energy and the shift into sunnier, brighter days. Therefore, Winter is a sacred time.

Winter's energy is one of going within so that our heart's desires and fresh inspirations can emerge. By consciously linking our awareness to nature's cycles, we find that our personal growth deepens.

> What's the point of stuffing down our darkness and hiding it? Negative emotions will arise at times. I suggest that, rather than labeling them as uncomfortable or even worse, that we are wrong for feeling them, we release

---

8. Chloë. "The Spiritual Significance of the Winter Solstice." exploredeeply.com. December 21, 2021. https://exploredeeply.com/live-your-purpose/winter-solstice-spiritual-meaning

them and focus on what we do want, rather than what we do not.

By fearing our own darkness, we stay stuck in it and detach from a powerful source of personal empowerment. Don't allow darkness to overwhelm your life and thoughts. Instead, recognize that darkness is a powerful catalyst for transformation. Do your best to revel in Winter Solstice's stillness prior to the Sun's strength growing and the days lengthening.

A major point to take note of here about Winter is that it's not the most opportune time to create shifts and change, or be in action. Instead, allow the energies of inspiration and new life, and ideas to slowly gestate within you. Before you know it, Spring will bring with it new growth that "springs" into manifestation!

Just as the seasons have their cycles, so do your personal growth and creations. Winter is the time to turn your capacity for compassion inward, to rest and reflect. Tremendous joy awaits you just around the corner in the New Year.[9]

Winter can be a challenging time, but there are simple ways to make your home more comfortable and enjoyable. To fight off the winter blues, try bringing more light into your space. This can be as easy as adding extra lamps or using candles. UV Lights and Sun Therapy is a great way to lift your spirits.

Making your home feel warmer doesn't just mean turning up the heat. Try placing soft blankets in easy-to-reach spots or keeping a basket of pine cones near your fireplace. Don't forget to keep your favorite mugs visible to remind you to enjoy warm, cozy drinks.

To maximize comfort, try rearranging your furniture. Create

9. Ibid.

inviting conversation areas by moving chairs and sofas closer together or towards the fireplace. You can even use big pillows on the floor for extra seating. The goal is to make your space more inviting since you'll likely be spending more time indoors. Remember, it's your home, so don't be afraid to make changes that help you feel more comfortable during the long winter months.

Susie's Top 11

1. Work - Work as if everything depends on you. Contribute and shift in your process of work. Build your team and delegate.
2. Think - Clearly focus on intentional and positive thoughts.
3. Play - Freely, and in a fun manner, let yourself be. Take in the pleasant moments.
4. Read - Alter your thoughts by learning and taking in new information.
5. Help - Help yourself, and others. Be kind and be strong.
6. Love - Love life. Love deeply. Be helpful and meaningful. Love as a verb and an action.
7. Dream - Dream big. Sit and imagine what you want. What you need. Dream big.
8. Laugh - Laugh often. Laugh loudly, with intention, and without restraint. Laughter helps heal.
9. Plan - This is the easiest to process. Plan to succeed.
10. Pray - Worship. Pray as if everything depends on it.
11. Restore - Restore activity. Spend time in the peaceful nature to restore. Passive rest to heal you, and mindfulness to stay present and practice being present.

Leadership Snack Pack

Teamwork Makes the Dreamwork

Be sure to build your dream team. Ignite your team. Activate your team. Delegate effectively and avoid getting in your own way.

Winter Checklist

EXERCISE

- Ask
- Listen
- Mirror back with authentic curiosity

TAKE ACTION

- What have you done so far?
- What can you do differently?
- What can you do better?
- What options do you have?
- What are you seriously considering
- Tell some stories that are relevant, that may be fun, or have an embedded lesson or analogy
- What would make you happy?
- What would make you at peace?
- What makes you sad?
- What makes you anxious?
- Also, ask them to consider the cost-benefits
- And then ask them what are the risks?
- Or so what?
- How does this make you feel?

- Mirror back joy smile eyes
- Tell them what they already know is going well and reaffirm this....
- Tell them what they already know is not going well and encourage them to find a solution.
- The answer is within them, and if it is not easily or readily retrievable, ask them to poll the audience....integrative thinking....the sum of others' input is better than your own

Conclusion Winter — The Season of Stillness and Strength

Winter arrives quietly, yet with an unmistakable presence. It is the season that invites leaders to slow down, to listen deeply, and to reconnect with what matters beneath the surface. While the world outside may feel cold or still, Winter is rich with internal movement—clarity forming, resilience strengthening, vision sharpening. Leadership in Winter is intentional, reflective, and steady. It is the season when wisdom grows roots.

In Winter, you are asked to rest without quitting, to think without rushing, and to plan without pressure. This is the time to conserve your energy, refine your direction, and honor the quiet work that fuels every future season. Winter reminds you that even in silence, transformation is happening.

As you close this chapter, imagine your own Winter, its calm, its depth, its quiet confidence. Let these reflections guide you as you cultivate inner strength.

Consider the following as you shape your Winter season:

Who is in your Winter circle?

Who brings calm, clarity, and grounding to your leadership? Who supports you in reflection, restoration, or long-term visioning?

What activities will you do?

What practices will help you recharge, learn, or reset, journaling, planning, reading, resting, or rebuilding systems?

Where will you do them?

Envision your Winter spaces, cozy corners, quiet offices, retreat settings, or peaceful outdoor paths where your mind slows and your thoughts settle.

What songs are playing?

What soundtrack suits your season of introspection? What music creates stillness, focus, or emotional warmth as you prepare for what's ahead?

Your Top 3 Tasks You Must Accomplish

Identify the three essential priorities that will define a purposeful Winter. What must be restored, reset, or reimagined before this season ends?

As you step into Winter, remember: this is the leadership season of stillness and strength. Let it steady you, renew you, and prepare you for the seasons yet to come.

From My Humble Rural Roots to Executive Leadership Coaching and Advisory Work

Wow. How did I get from the rural Prairie to the Bay Street Board Room? I sometimes wonder if it was always meant to be. My path may have been predetermined. I have always loved people. I am curious in nature, and I come from a long line of storytellers. I love a good story, and I appreciate cool and interesting characters.

As a former underdog, I truly enjoy helping others to get the wolves off the doorstep, and to help others find a way forward when all seems impossible.

How did this start? It was by chance, or so it seemed. Vistage (TEC) contacted me via LinkedIn. Sounded like a scam. Far from it. It was better than I could have ever imagined. Upon reviewing, I determined this was the real deal. Well at least I hoped it was. I asked friends and colleagues and a few trusted folks told me to go for it.

Through that, I discovered this might be my true calling. Although I was skeptical, I decided I would explore it further. I attended the Vistage Academy in 2018, launched my first coaching group in 2019, and have not looked back. Of course, I've had lots of twists and turns. Some lows, some highs. I was named Canada's Top Gun in 2019. I won many crystal trophies for coaching, including Excellence Awards, Launch Awards, and, my favourite highlight, Master Chair Status.

One of my favourite highs was my chance meeting with Marshall Goldsmith. I quickly realized we had a similar thought process and I started coaching training with him.

I realized on my coaching journey, having a formal coaching certification would also carry me further than most. The Stakeholder Centered Coaching methods developed by Goldsmith resonated most with me. I decided during Covid to complete my Stakeholder Centered Coaching education through Marshall Goldsmith.

So I am very proud to say I am a certified coach and the Marshall Goldsmith method has served me in coaching my clients to success

The Vistage International and TEC Canada Community has been all I hoped it would be and more, and the Marshall Goldsmith Methods of Stakeholder Centered coaching have provided me with a firm foundation.

The onset of the COVID-19 lockdowns triggered a really deep low for me as a single mom, working from home virtually, with two school-age kids, no nannies, no programs, no help. I tried everything to keep my family afloat. Some very good people helped me, and I did find the occasional wolf on my doorstep. I can honestly say that my community mattered the most in times of need. I activated my network, I prayed a lot, I looked inward and outward for a path forward and I found my way by the grace of God. I am stronger and wiser because of my journey.

The good thing about me is that I've walked the journey from nowhere to somewhere and everything in between.

I'm really looking forward to the future, and can barely wait to see what life has in store for me next.

Bringing It All Together

We need to be curious, ask questions, and be an active listener. Thankful heart and gratitude go a long way.

Be sure to thank your Seasonal Circle for feed-forward input.

What do you need to stop, start, and continue to advance your goal? Incremental steps make a huge impact over the long run.

Collaboration, stakeholders, and a thoughtful executable plan goes a long way. Adding feedforward input and incremental, actionable change will have lasting effects.

Reconnecting family, work, and community is possible when you take a holistic, authentic approach. Consider your Seasonal Circle.

Ask, Listen, Thank, Act. A system created by Marshall Goldsmith, which goes as follows;

Ask: Ask people for specific, future-focused advice on how you can better your job, role or relationship.

Listen: Listen to the feedback with respect and without judgment. Demonstrate engagement through eye contact and body language.

Think: Take time to process the feedback. Consider what it means and how you can apply it.

Feedback is Crucial: Goldsmith emphasizes that continuous, confidential feedback from stakeholders is vital for leadership development and for assessing whether one is improving.

Focus on Behavior: Successful leaders recognize that, as they advance, their greatest challenges are behavioral. The process helps them address these behaviors directly.

Act on What You Learn: The most important part is translating the feedback into action. Without acting on the feedback, the process has no impact.

LEADERSHIP MUST-DO LIST

- Be innovative
- Be courageous
- Have integrity
- Be honest
- Be compassionate
- Be present
- Be aware
- Be calm
- Be focused
- Be clear
- Have inner peace
- Be positive
- Listen more
- Be consistent
- Have integrity
- Have perseverance
- Be inspired
- Be a hope dealer
- Be curious

- Ask more questions
- Be an active listener
- Have gratitude
- Say thanks and give grace
- Restart, reset, refocus.
- Don't give up.
- Trust, allow and receive.

For the College Graduate

I wish every new graduate, every new employee, and every new teammate could receive this list, carry it with them, and read it every day. Maybe put it on the visor of their car, in their wallet or beside their bed, or taped to their bathroom mirror. This is the list to live by. It does work. It will elevate you and everyone else around you.

Seasonal Success Checklist

☐ Set clear, achievable goals for each season

- Define specific objectives for work, family, and personal growth
- Ensure goals are SMART (Specific, Measurable, Achievable, Relevant, Time-bound)
- Align goals with overall vision and long-term plans

☐ Create an executable plan with your team

- Break down goals into actionable steps
- Assign responsibilities and set deadlines
- Identify potential obstacles and plan mitigation strategies

☐ Delegate tasks and monitor progress

- Empower team members by matching tasks to their strengths
- Establish regular check-ins to track advancement
- Provide necessary resources and support for success

☐ Regularly reflect and reassess

- Schedule time for personal and team reflection
- Analyze what's working well and what needs improvement
- Be open to feedback and new ideas from team members

☐ Be prepared to adjust plans as needed

- Stay flexible and adaptable to changing circumstances
- Develop contingency plans for potential setbacks
- Embrace change as an opportunity for growth and innovation

☐ Establish rituals for rest and connection

- Create a relaxing bedtime routine to improve sleep quality
- Plan regular family meals or activities to strengthen bonds
- Designate tech-free times to encourage genuine interaction

☐ Choose shared activities/series to enjoy with family

- Select a TV series, book, or podcast to experience together

- Plan outdoor winter activities like sledding or ice skating
- Start a family project or hobby to work on throughout the season

☐ Practice being present without distractions

- Set aside dedicated time for mindfulness or meditation
- Engage fully in conversations without checking devices
- Focus on sensory experiences in your environment

☐ Make time for restoration and reflection

- Schedule regular self-care activities like baths or massages
- Keep a winter journal to process thoughts and emotions
- Create a cozy space for quiet contemplation

☐ Balance work commitments with personal time

- Set clear boundaries between work and personal life
- Use vacation days for genuine rest and rejuvenation
- Learn to say no to non-essential commitments

Leadership Checklist

☐ Lead with a calm, steady hand

- Maintain composure during stressful situations
- Communicate clearly and confidently to inspire trust
- Model the behavior and attitude you expect from your team

☐ Address problems proactively

- Anticipate potential issues before they escalate
- Encourage open communication about challenges
- Develop solutions collaboratively with team members

☐ Create a positive work rhythm

- Establish productive routines and workflows
- Balance periods of intense focus with restorative breaks
- Celebrate team achievements and milestones regularly

☐ Delegate effectively without abdicating responsibility

- Match tasks to team members' strengths and development goals
- Provide clear instructions and expectations for delegated work
- Offer support and guidance while allowing autonomy

☐ Build trust through consistency

- Follow through on commitments and promises
- Apply policies and standards fairly across the team
- Be transparent about decision-making processes

Community Building Checklist

☐ Identify local issues needing attention

- Conduct community surveys or town hall meetings
- Analyze local data and trends to spot emerging problems
- Listen to diverse voices, especially from marginalized groups

☐ Assemble diverse stakeholder teams

- Include representatives from various community sectors
- Seek out individuals with different perspectives and experiences
- Ensure all team members have equal opportunity to contribute

☐ Create actionable plans with clear goals

- Develop specific, measurable objectives for community improvement
- Break down large initiatives into manageable steps
- Assign responsibilities and set realistic timelines

☐ Monitor progress and adapt as needed

- Establish regular check-ins to assess advancement
- Use data and feedback to evaluate effectiveness of initiatives
- Be willing to adjust strategies based on new information or challenges

☐ Celebrate successes and milestones

- Recognize both small wins and major achievements
- Share success stories with the wider community
- Use celebrations as opportunities to build momentum and engagement

Workplace Environment Checklist

☐ Assess comfort and functionality of spaces

- Evaluate ergonomics of workstations and common areas
- Consider lighting, temperature, and noise levels
- Seek feedback from employees on their workspace needs

☐ Ensure proper tools and resources are available

- Regularly update technology and software as needed
- Provide necessary training for efficient use of tools
- Create systems for easy access to information and resources

☐ Create inviting break areas

- Design comfortable spaces for relaxation and social interaction
- Offer healthy snacks and beverages
- Include elements that promote stress relief (e.g., plants, art)

☐ Implement meaningful rituals and traditions

- Establish regular team-building activities or celebrations
- Create routines that reinforce company values and culture
- Encourage employee-led initiatives for workplace community

☐ Regularly gather feedback for improvements

- Conduct anonymous surveys on workplace satisfaction
- Hold open forums for suggestions and concerns
- Act on feedback to show employees their input is valued

Personal Growth Checklist

☐ Set goals for mind, body, and spirit

- Define specific objectives for intellectual, physical, and emotional growth
- Create a balanced plan that addresses all aspects of well-being
- Align personal goals with your values and long-term vision

☐ Seek out new learning opportunities

- Identify skills or knowledge areas you want to develop
- Explore courses, workshops, or mentorship programs
- Challenge yourself to step outside your comfort zone regularly

☐ Practice gratitude daily

- Keep a gratitude journal to record positive experiences
- Express appreciation to others more frequently
- Reflect on lessons learned from challenges and setbacks

☐ Take time for self-reflection

- Schedule regular "check-ins" with yourself
- Analyze your progress towards goals and personal growth
- Identify areas for improvement and celebrate achievements

☐ Celebrate small wins and progress

- Acknowledge and reward yourself for completing tasks or reaching milestones
- Share your accomplishments with supportive friends or family
- Use small successes as motivation to tackle bigger challenges

I found this poem hidden behind my kitchen wall while renovating my old log cabin. There it sat, hidden for decades hanging on the logs, sandwiched between the old paneling in my kitchen, and the ridiculously old logs.

I thought it was a perfect closing poem for my book as it captures the very essence of goodness, space, time, nature and God.

Read this poem often. It will help you for sure. It helps me calmly approach my days.

Slow me down, Lord
Ease the pounding of my heart by the quieting of my mind.
Steady my hurried pace with a vision of eternal reach of time.
Give me, amid the confusion of the day, the calmness of the everlasting hills.
Break the tensions of my nerves and muscles with the soothing music of the singing streams that live in my memory. Help me to know the magical, restoring power of sleep.
Teach me the art of taking minute vacations - of slowing down to look at a flower, to chat with a friend, to pat a dog, to read a few lines from a good book.
Slow me down, Lord, and inspire me to send my roots

deep into the soil of life's enduring values that I may grow towards the stars of my greater destiny.

— *WILFRED A. PETERSON*

ABOUT THE AUTHOR

Susan Motkaluk was born in a tiny town in rural Manitoba into an impoverished farming family. Through relentless hard work and an unwavering commitment to excellence, she rose to become a respected executive and leadership coach with a track record of delivering meaningful, lasting change.

Susan earned a Bachelor of Applied Science in Civil Engineering (Honours) from the University of Waterloo, then her Professional Engineering designation, laying the foundation for a career that would span both public and private sector leadership. Over the years she has held senior roles and both Chief Administrative Officer and Chief Executive Officer, consistently driving innovation and results.

During her time as CAO, Susan spearheaded the revitalization of a downtown business district, leading to record-breaking development activity between 2011 and 2015. Later, as CEO, she designed a bold 10-year strategy that introduced a community hub-based model for long term care facilities, reshaping how care homes connect with the communities they serve.

Susan was recipient of TEC Canada's Top Gun accolade in 2019. Her Community Development work has earned international acclaim, including designation by the United Nations as a Global Good Practice, and the Dubai International Award for best practices in improving the living environment.

A TEC Canada and Vistage International Master Chair, and Marshall Goldsmith Stakeholder Centered Certified Coach, Susan now partners with senior leaders, blending strategic insight with the wisdom of nature's seasons and her own remarkable journey.

BEFORE YOU GO

If you found this book helpful and enjoyed it, I would really appreciate it if you would please leave a short review on Amazon. It really helps me, and it will bring these life-changing tools and tips into the hands of more people. Your ratings and reviews will increase this book's visibility in the algorithm, making it more discoverable.

Thank you in advance for this generous expression of your appreciation. Your reviews will encourage me to spend more time sharing my advice with the public.

You can also email me directly with your thoughts at:
Susan@sdminc.ca

Thank you for reading and thank you for being the kind of person who helps others by sharing what you've learned.

Made in the USA
Coppell, TX
18 June 2026

81319589R00115